ROUTLEDGE LIBRARY EDITIONS:
ENVIRONMENTAL AND NATURAL
RESOURCE ECONOMICS

Volume 4

THE POLITICAL ECONOMY OF
SMOG IN SOUTHERN CALIFORNIA

THE POLITICAL ECONOMY OF SMOG IN SOUTHERN CALIFORNIA

JEFFRY FAWCETT

LONDON AND NEW YORK

First published in 1990 by Garland Publishing, Inc.

This edition first published in 2018
by Routledge
2 Park Square, Milton Park, Abingdon, Oxon OX14 4RN

and by Routledge
711 Third Avenue, New York, NY 10017

Routledge is an imprint of the Taylor & Francis Group, an informa business

British Library Cataloguing in Publication Data
A catalogue record for this book is available from the British Library

ISBN: 978-1-138-08283-0 (Set)
ISBN: 978-1-315-14775-8 (Set) (ebk)
ISBN: 978-1-138-08346-2 (Volume 4) (hbk)
ISBN: 978-1-315-11226-8 (Volume 4) (ebk)

Publisher's Note
The publisher has gone to great lengths to ensure the quality of this reprint but
points out that some imperfections in the original copies may be apparent.

Disclaimer
The publisher has made every effort to trace copyright holders and would welcome
correspondence from those they have been unable to trace.

THE POLITICAL ECONOMY
OF SMOG IN
SOUTHERN CALIFORNIA

JEFFRY FAWCETT

Garland Publishing, Inc.
NEW YORK & LONDON 1990

Library of Congress Cataloging-in-Publication Data

Fawcett, Jeffry.
The political economy of smog in southern California / Jeffry Fawcett.
p. cm. — (The Environment—problems and solutions)
Includes bibliographical references.
ISBN 0-8240-2525-3 (alk. paper)
1. Air—Pollution—Economic aspects—California, Southern.
2. Environmental policy—California, Southern. 3. Saving and investment—
California, Southern. 4. Capitalism—California, Southern. I. Title. II.
Series.
HC107.C23A44 1990
363.73'87—dc20   90-45456

PRINTED IN THE UNITED STATES OF AMERICA

Dedicated to the memory of my grandmother
Carmen (Dake) Critchlow
who quit smoking in her eighties.
There is hope for us all.

And very specially dedicated to my best friend
Margo Hendricks
who deserves more than a book dedicated to her.

CONTENTS

The Political Economy Of Smog
In Southern California

CHAPTER 1

Political Economy

Southern California is famous for air pollution. For over forty years

Figure 1-1
The physiographic boundaries of the South Coast Air Basin and California counties

the political institutions of the South Coast Air Basin (Figure 1-1) have attempted to deal effectively with the smog issue. Because of this long history, and because this history is so characteristic of modern environmental regulation, the political economy of smog in Southern

California is a microcosm of the political economy of environmental regulation in Post-World War II America.

Like the vast majority of environmental issues to emerge since World War II, the political economy of smog in Southern California features technical discovery, policy innovation and institutional change. But all of this discovery, innovation and change have taken place against the backdrop of Southern California's emergence as the center of corporate capitalism on the Pacific Rim.[1] Among the social and political superstructures supporting the economic structure of Southern California growth are those which shape the knowledge, debate and decisionmaking that determine how clean the air is. The conclusion of this study is that the institutions affecting air quality in Southern California, as with all superstructural institutions, function to abet the accumulation of capital and the material form of capitalist development.

This conclusion is in contrast to the orientation of the vast majority of the literature in environmental economics. The field of environmental economics and policy study is dominated by applied neoclassical microeconomic theory.[2] The contrasting position I take in here is that of institutional and marxist economics—traditions which are virtually unheard of in environmental analysis.[3] As a consequence, this first chapter is spent contrasting these two different kinds of economic analysis, which I will characterize as utilitarian (mainstream, neoclassical) and functionalist (institutionalist and marxist) political economy.

At the heart of this study is my concern for how institutions can succeed or fail at environmental improvement. This is a common enough concern of political economists. However, I do not approach the question of effective institutional arrangements from a purely formal standpoint, such as the abstract neoclassical models involving market mechanisms. Instead, I look first at the nature of environmental politics and the history of air pollution control in Southern California. I then develop a political economic model that asks a simple question: what effect have the dramatic changes that have occurred throughout the history of air pollution control in Southern California had on air quality? The point of asking the question is twofold: to evaluate the relationship between air quality and institutional change; and to evaluate how political economists explain (and consequently prescribe) how state environmental institutions work.

POLITICAL ECONOMISTS

The institutions of greatest interest in this study are the public ones, and particularly local regulatory agencies, which have nominally dominated the political economy of smog in Southern California. The mainstream economics literature has the apt caption of public choice. The key contrast between utilitarian and functionalist analysis is in the treatment of how the public makes choices, how choices are made over the supply of public goods, and how choices are made in public.

The utilitarian view is that the social landscape consists of a network of intentional acts, represented most accurately by the concept of the dynamic equilibrium of the supply of and demand for public and private goods. Public choice is the pursuit and satisfaction of preferences for goods which can be supplied through public institutions. Positive reform takes place when institutions economize on the pursuit and satisfaction of such preferences. However, the real content of the choice is external to the utilitarian model—utilitarian analysis concerns itself only with the form of choice, not with its content.

The functionalist view is that the network of intentional acts is overlaid with a pattern intended to promote the domination of capitalist economic relations. The form and content of public choice are inseparable because the pattern of institutional arrangements is intended to privilege some choices, taint others and preclude still others.

A point of agreement between these two modes of analysis is the dysfunctionality of current institutional arrangements for environmental improvement. The contrast in explanation for this dysfunctionality, however, further points up the contrast between the utilitarian and functionalist forms of analysis. For the utilitarian, the institutions of environmental improvement do not work well because the institutions do not have the right structural relationship with the underlying causes of pollution. For the functionalist, the institutions of environmental improvement do not work because that is not what they are intended to do. What they are intended to do is to prevent the abatement of capital accumulation and the material development that embodies accumulation.

Illustrative of the contrast between these two approaches is the life cycle theory of regulation. Authors such as Anthony Downs and Barry Mitnick espouse a theory of regulatory process in terms of stages[4]—regulatory institutions have identifiable if not precisely demarcated boundaries during their institutional lifetime. Robert Doty based his dissertation on the development of air pollution control in Los Angeles County in terms of the life cycle theory.[5]

What can be said in favor of this biological analogy is that the unit of analysis is the system as a whole. The weakness is in the treatment of the underlying "metabolic" processes that are the immediate cause of the life cycle itself. In the case of life cycle theories of regulation—and virtually all other economic theories of regulation[6]—the analysis is in terms of how individual 'phenotypes' exploit their environment through the pursuit of what they perceive to be their self-interest. A good ecological analogy would look instead at how institutions exploit individual 'phenotypes' in order to achieve stability, growth and development. That is, the contrast between individual choice and the pattern of choice.

Each of the three traditions in political economics—neoclassical, institutionalist and marxist[7]—is based on the hypothesis that people act in their own self interest. What distinguishes the utilitarian from the functionalist tradition is the meaning of "self interest" and the way in which actions based on self interest affect and are affected by social institutions.

Neoclassical political economists take interests as more or less given through utility functions and treat all institutions (or at least the economically relevant ones) as ultimately reducible to exchange relationships—i.e., institutional dynamics are fundamentally the dynamics of supply and demand.[8] Utility functions describe the psychological causes of choice. Exchange relations are the ratiocinations of choice.

Institutionalist political economists take interests not as given but as being affected by institutional dynamics—i.e., interests are shaped. In turn, institutional dynamics may be viewed as reducible to a kind of exchange, but a profoundly unequal form of exchange. An important distinction is made by institutionalists between supply/demand dynamics and processes involving the exercise of power and control.[9] Marxist political economists, like institutionalists, take interests not as a datum but as a product of institutional dynamics.

What distinguishes marxists from institutionalists is their characterization of these institutional dynamics. Marxists, like institutionalists, focus on how individuals and classes (particularly elites) use institutions to achieve their goals. In addition, marxists look at the way in which institutions work to fulfill the interests of the dominant class without regard to the specific actions taken by the members of these elites.[10] The meaning of "elite" for marxists is also more specific than for institutionalists--namely, "elite" is defined exclusively as the owners of the means of production and their agents.[11]

John Maguire describes Marx's thought dramaturgically:

> The owning class, as it were, own the theatre, but they do not write the script—indeed there is no settled script—so that the drama frequently gets out of hand. This is chiefly because there is a section of the chorus who want a completely different production, and are acquiring the power to impose it.[12]

The kind of reforms that each family of political economist is concerned with tends to fall along equally identifiable lines. Utilitarians want to reform public institutions so they more closely approximate market institutions. Functionalists want to reform public and private institutions so that the market power of elites is less easily translated into political power or done away with altogether. Oddly enough, both traditions do so with the hope of improving welfare.

A convenient, if vague way to refer to these concerns with explanation and reform is to say that political economists are concerned with the rules of the game. 'Rules of the game' has two meanings. The most obvious sense is the explicit and implicit rules that individuals follow when public decisions are made. These are the rules of the institutional game that is being analyzed.

The second sense of 'rules of the game' concern the rules of the explanation game. Like any other kind of scientist, the political economist is not only concerned with explaining why certain events occur, but also with what counts as a good explanation.

For the neoclassical economist, good explanations of public institutions account for political outcomes by referring to how individuals respond to the incentives that the institutions create. Public institutions work well when the incentives cause people to act in ways that improve welfare, defined as improvements in their ability to fulfill the interests defined by their utility functions. Institutional change is a change in these incentives. The change is positive when individuals are able to fulfill more of their interests or economize on the fulfillment.

For the institutionalists and marxists, good explanations of public institutions account for political outcomes by referring to the bias inherent in the institution. The bias is of two kinds. First, members of elites have advantageous access to the use of the institutions to fulfill their interest. And second, the rules of the institutional game are designed so that outcomes favor elites, whether they actually use their disproportionate access or not. Institutions work well when outcomes conform to general interests. Institutional change occurs when the bias of the institution changes. Change is positive when the power of the dominant class is minimized.

EXPLANATION

When Willie Sutton was in prison, a priest who was trying to reform him asked him why he robbed banks. "Well," Sutton replied, "that's where the money is."[13]

The anecdote is used by Alan Garfinkel in *Forms Of Explanation* to demonstrate the dynamics of explanation. The humor in the brief tale comes from the apparent misunderstanding between the priest and Sutton: the priest is asking one question ("Why do you rob [instead of not rob] banks?"), whereas Sutton answers another question ("Why do you rob banks [instead of other kinds of things]?").

Garfinkel argues that this kind of (mis)understanding is at the bottom of how we form and respond to explanations. Sutton and the priest view different aspects of Sutton's behavior as needing explanation, and hence have in mind a different set of alternatives or actions when they say what they say: Sutton [robs / does not rob] banks; Sutton robs [banks / other things].

The story illustrates what Garfinkel calls explanatory relativity: explanations are always given with a limited set of alternatives in mind, and more importantly with a particular view as to what is problematic about a given event or situation. Garfinkel calls this set of alternatives, and the corresponding view of what is problematic, an explanatory space.

For the neoclassical economist, what is problematic about environmental regulation is the failure of state institutions to create the exchange relations required to achieve the welfare maximizing outcome. The utilitarian form of explanation looks for that social outcome which makes everyone as well off as they can be. People are as well off as they can be when they have use of the resources at their disposal (initial endowments) to satisfy what they perceive to be their needs (described by utility functions). State institutions hinder the natural bargaining process by imposing agents in the process who have the wrong incentives. The incentives of regulators have little to do with achieving an environmentally optimum outcome. The regulator's incentives have to do with career advancement, prestige, monetary reward and other goals irrelevant to environmental quality.[14]

What is problematic from a functionalist perspective is how the bias of state institutions toward the interests of the dominant class can be abated. Part of the problem is that the dominant class uses its superior position to maintain its superior position. The other part of the problem is that the institutional bias prevents the full recognition and realization of interests. Even with bargaining arrangements, the outcome would still not be optimal because the process, along with what each side brings to the bargain, biases the outcome.

A striking example of the difference can be found in classic work by Baumol and Oates, *The Theory of Environmental Policy*.[15] They devote an entire chapter to the relationship between the distribution of income and the demand for environmental quality, recognizing the correlation between high income and increased demand for environmental quality. What is surprising is that the use of income redistribution is never discussed as an instrument of environmental reform. The line of argument instead follows a path which sets up an inherent conflict between environmental improvement and income distribution as goals of state institutions. In discussing the economic impact of environmental regulation, presumed to be pervasively negative, Baumol and Oates exemplify the utilitarian model:

What this [analysis] suggests to us is the need to incorporate sensible redistributive provisions into environmental programs, both as a matter of justice and as a means to enhance their political feasibility. We should not, however, lose sight of the fact *that the primary purpose of environmental programs is allocative:* their basic rationale is the direction of resource use to achieve desired levels of environmental quality.[16]

A Garfinkel-like question / contrast can focus the difference. Both utilitarian and functionalist will ask: Why do state institutions fail to maximize environmental improvement? For the utilitarian this means: why do [state institutions fail to / market institutions succeed in] maximize environmental improvement? For the functionalist the question / contrast means: why do state institutions [fail to maximize environmental improvement / succeed in preserving and promoting basic economic social relations]?

In criticizing mainstream political economic theories of regulation, Victor Goldberg puts the case succinctly.

The fundamental principle of economics is that people will pursue their own self-interest within a given institutional framework. The economist's basic policy premise is that...this self-interest will, like an Invisible Hand, guide resources to their proper usage; when market failures arise the usual policy prescription is to amend the rules to make the marginal private costs and benefits equal to the marginal social costs and benefits.... But this picture imposes an arbitrary demarcation on the boundaries of self-interest: not only will people pursue their self-interest *within* the rules; they will also allocate resources toward *changing* the rules to their own benefit.[17]

FUNCTIONALIST EXPLANATION

Both the utilitarian and functionalist critique of state institutions is structural. The structure of a thing is defined by the relationship among its parts.

> The structure of an argument is given by the relations between its constituent statements, of a bridge by the relations between its constituent girders,spans, etc. (for short: parts). The statements and parts belong to the argument and bridge, but not to their respective structures. . . . There is no difficulty extending these remarks to the case of the economic structure and its constituent relations. . . . The structure may be seen not only as a set of relations but also as a set of roles.[18]

The relevant roles for the utilitarian are the exchange based roles of consumer / buyer and producer / supplier / seller. The characteristics of these roles are fully described by utility functions, production functions and initial endowments. The objective in role performance for each individual person is simply to exploit the resources at her disposal in a series of exchanges so that she ends up with more than she started out with. "More" in this context mean more in value terms—the person likes the bundle of stuff she ends up with better than the bundle of stuff she started out with.

The functionalist view is that the goal of possession and consumption of the utilitarian is a result and not the basis of economic and social activity. The content of the exchanges that so concern the utilitarian are dominated by the level of income and the social status associated with class position. The relevant roles are defined by the economic structure in terms of the power an individual has over income-producing property and over his own capacity to work.[19] The basic roles are comprised of an owning class (own means of production and command their own labor power and that of others), a working class (own no means of production and have no control over their own labor power or the labor power of other[20]) and a professional class (who own no or very little in the way of means of production but who do control their own labor power and perhaps the labor power of others).[21]

> A person's class is established by nothing but his objective place in the network of ownership relations, however difficult it may be to identify such places neatly. His consciousness, culture, and politics do not enter the *definition* of his class position....The connection between production relations on the one hand and consciousness, politics, and culture on the other is not simple. There is logic in it but not law.[22]

This implies two things. First, the relationship between class and political action is not a simple transformation of one into the other. Second, the nature of the transformation is explained functionally. As G.A. Cohen puts it, the base needs the superstructure: the actual performance of the relevant social roles are called forth by the more fundamental forces of the economic structure.

Functional explanation is commonly used in the life sciences, but is at best controversial in the social sciences. Some examples of functional explanations:

> Cats have large canine teeth because large canine teeth facilitate the capture and holding of prey.

> Monarch butterflies have the markings of Viceroy butterflies because such markings trick potential predators into thinking the tasty Monarch is an undesirable Viceroy.

Statements that are intended to be functional explanations are of the form 'The function of x is to d.' Functional explanation consists in the claim that 'The function of x is to d' explains why x occurred (when explaining an event) or why x exists (when explaining a state of affairs or state of being).

To many, the use of functional explanation in the social science, and even in the natural sciences, is not considered a legitimate form of explanation. The argument against functional explanation goes something like this: 'the function of a society's rituals is to preserve social cohesion' looks like 'the function of my participation in the Masonic Lodge is to establish business contacts'; however, natural persons can have intentions, act purposefully and act with the expectation of future benefits, but a society cannot. That is, the effect of an event cannot be used to explain that event. The only situation in which this works is in explaining the actions of the kinds of things that have intentions.

There are two responses to this criticism. A weak response is that institutions may not "really" have intentions, but the treatment of institutions as if they did have intentions yields useful explanatory models. A strong response denies the terms of the criticism.

A critique of the utilitarian concept of externality is an example of the strong response. An externality[23] is any cost or benefit imposed on someone not directly involved in an activity, where the effect is external to the purpose of the activity. If I live next to a flower nursery, the fragrance that blows in through my windows free of charge is an external benefit of living in that location: the owner of the nursery does not intend to serve up those fragrances, but is instead intent on selling flowers. And if I live next to a freeway, the automobile effluents that blow in through the window free of charge, and increase the risk that I will suffer from diminished respiratory function, are an external cost of my living in that location: the owners of the automobiles drive to reach a destination, not to give me emphysema.

Environmental degradation is a classic externality. Environmental degradation is external to the production process: pollution is an unintended result of production and consumption decisions. It is not because corporate decisionmakers do not care about environmental quality. Rather, it is because performing their role as industrial managers does not call for them to consider environmental quality. Environmental degradation is very relevant to the creation of goods, but irrelevant to the accumulation of capital and therefore is intentionally not included as a goal of production.[24]

Institutions consist of a set of roles defined by social relations and occupied by particular people. Institutions have their effect through the activity of these people. People act purposefully in pursuing a number of objectives among which is the performance of their role. People may perform that role correctly or incorrectly, well or badly. What determines the adequacy of their performance is not their intentions nor what they think of their actions, but how others evaluate and respond to their actions. And the purpose of the institution may have nothing to do with any of the intentions of those who occupy roles:

Adam Smith's invisible hand is paradigmatic. In neoclassical theory, the function of markets is to allocate resources.[25]

If institutions have a function, then they can fulfill that function well or badly. Both utilitarian and functionalist political economists agree that environmental institutions are dysfunctional from a welfare standpoint. But from the functionalist perspective, the function of these institutions is to maintain the power of the dominant class is fulfilled.

POWER

Steven Lukes[26] distinguishes three dimensions of social power—three ways in which a person or social group can have their way at the expense of another. One dimensional power is the ability of a person or group to prevail over others in a decisionmaking situation involving observable conflicts of interest. Lukes criticizes this view for failing to account for situations in which power is exercised in the determination of what actually will see the light of day in a decisionmaking situation involving observable conflicts of interest.

This latter, agenda-setting power is Lukes' second dimension of power. Power is exercised when potential issues involving observable conflicts of interest are prevented from being addressed by an appropriate decisionmaking process. This kind of power is clearly an extension of one-dimensional power from public forums (where nominally everyone has equal access) to private and quasi-public forums (where access is unequal).

The distinctive feature of the first two dimensions of power is that they involve the intentional actions of some person or group pursuing their interests. G. William Domhoff's *The Powers That Be*[27] describes four processes that illustrate these two dimensions of power: the special interest process, the policy formation process, the candidate selection process and the ideology process. In neoclassical terms, these two dimensions of power can be reduced to a set of resource allocations. Political actors enter the bargaining for goods supplied through public institutions with ability to pursue a particular goal (i.e., initial endowments such as money, time and political acumen) and the willingness to pursue that goal (i.e., preferences for the goods described by utility functions and production functions). In institutionalist and marxist terms, these two dimensions of power are described as instrumental power, where the owning class uses the various agencies of the state as an instrument to achieve their goals.

Lukes criticizes the two dimensional view of power on three grounds. First, he maintains that non-decisionmaking is a form of decisionmaking. The two dimensional view focusses on the conscious exercise of power, while ignoring institutionalized power which is not attributable to the conscious will of any person or group. Second, he criticizes the two dimensional view for its preoccupation with observable conflict because it fails to address the exercise of power through manipulation, the appeal to authority and other means used to prevent conflict from arising. And third, Lukes says that the two dimensional view fails to address the shaping of interests themselves, where power is exercised by preventing classes of people from recognizing or being aware of what policies would be in their interests.

Domhoff's processes—particularly the policy formation and ideology processes—describe in a more limited extent the third dimension of power. The third dimension of power Lukes describes partakes of functionalist explanation. Unlike the first two dimensions, the third dimension of power promotes or precludes issues without the intentional action of the people who benefit from a particular decision or action. The first two dimensions of power more or less assume that the institutional structure itself is neutral. The three dimensional view (like functionalist theory) assumes that the institutional structure is biased toward particular classes. This lack of bias is in addition to the differences in the ability of affected groups to marshall the resources necessary to prevail within that structure.

Matthew Crenson's study, *The Un-Politics Of Air Pollution: A Study Of Non-Decisionmaking In The Cities*[28], is cited by Lukes as showing the third dimensional of power. Crenson's book is a comparative study of the issue in Gary, Indiana and East Chicago, Indiana. Crenson's thesis is that although the two cities 'looked' alike, air pollution control came later to Gary because the issue never got on the political agenda. Despite citizen activism equivalent to that in East Chicago, Gary adopted an air pollution ordinance a decade after East

Chicago because the issue was ignored by the City Council and local industry. Edward Greer[29] later criticized Crenson's thesis. As an insider to Gary City Hall decisionmaking, Greer claims that two dimensional power could explain what occurred—the City Council was being directly lobbied by industrialists to prevent air pollution from becoming an issue in Gary; and the Council and Office of the Mayor (Richard Hatcher) intentionally refused to raise the issue.[30]

This point reflects a conflict from within the marxist tradition: the conflict between the view that government institutions *per se* are neutral (with the evil perpetrated by them explainable by the independent power of the ruling class) and the view that they are inherently biased. In the former case, the evils visited upon citizens are the result of the independent power of the ruling class to have its way. In the latter case, the evils can and do occur without the direct intervention of the ruling class. Arguments ensue over the reform of capitalist institutions. On the one hand, there is the view that state institutions can be used to obtain the correct outcomes by replacing "bad guys" with "good guys"—maintain the institutional relations but occupy the roles with people not beholden to or insensitive to the demands of the dominant class. On the other hand, there is the view that both the people and the roles have to be changed.[31]

The debate itself revolves around issues somewhat removed from the discussion here (i.e., the appropriate form of public decisionmaking in a socialist society on its way to becoming a communist society). What concerns us here is how much the development, change and stability of environmental institutions can be explained by who occupies a role and how much depends on the characteristics of the role itself. This latter includes how those role characteristics are maintained despite a change in the person who occupies the role—a new person with a new utility function to describe her values, interests and intentions.

The concept of hegemony[32] concentrates on the way in which the institutions in capitalist societies are interwoven so that they reinforce one another. The concept of hegemony also draws attention to the ways in which subjugated classes forced to act against their own interest through the domination of these institutions. Hegemony is not the same as complete or absolute domination—where the will or interests of one class unilaterally and unequivocally prevails in all cases.

The capitalist state and other superstructural institutions perform two basic functions.[33] First, these institutions maintain the cohesiveness of the owning class and promote the interests of the owning class as whole, despite conflicts between the interests of particular members and the class as a whole.[34] Second, these institutions perform the apparently more mundane function of maintaining social stability and minimizing conflict.[35]

Maintaining law and order is only apparently mundane; imbedded in this function of the state is the more pernicious one of reinforcing behavior and norms that minimize conflict, and do so in ways that are biased toward owning class interests. This concept and the associated marxist concepts of ideology and of alienation provide the material difference between utilitarian and functionalist explanations.

Utilitarian explanations account for the structure of public decisionmaking solely in terms of utility functions, production functions and exchange relations. Four interconnected theses form the basis of utilitarian explanation. First is the assumption that human beings act in their own interests. Second is that these interests are defined in terms of the consequences of the person's actions. Third, the evaluation of these consequences is subjected to some sort of rational calculus. And fourth, people will exploit whatever means are available in pursuing their interests.[36]

Functionalist explanations account for the structure of public decisionmaking in terms of interests (utility functions), market power (production *cum* profit functions and income) and hegemonic power (the ability to define, for example, what is and is not an issue). Self-interested action has its place in functionalist explanation and in fact plays a prominent explanatory role[37]—with the important caveat that people act in their own interests *as they see them*.[38] Values have to do with a person's self-perception (state-of-being) rather than with their possessions (state-of-having). Also called second-order interests, these may be thought of as organizing the arguments in utility functions—for example, the adoption of a professional code of ethics or the adoption of a particular consumption pattern in clothing or housing as an extension of performing properly in a given profession or social role.

The marxist concept of ideology is distinguished from this notion of second and higher order interests by its character as false consciousness—i.e., a self-awareness or set of second-order interests that prevent the articulation of some, potentially more fundamental set of real interests.[39] The concept of alienation is what explains, in the marxist theory, the existence of this false consciousness.[40] People play roles as members of a particular class in a specific kind of power relationship with members of another class. The roles that individuals find themselves forced to play call forth the kinds of second order interests that make performance of the role psychologically and morally possible for the individual person.[41] Alienation occurs because these second-order interests are functional only with respect to the existence of hegemonic and subordinate classes. The corollary is that there exists a set of real interests that the members of these classes possess but which are masked by the continuation of the hegemonic social structure.

In utilitarian explanations the person is seen as one thing: a utility maximizer. Regardless of the sophistication with which this view is applied, there is in utilitarian theory a unity between what a person experiences and the actions that this person takes.[42] In functionalist explanation the person is two things: an objective self and a subjective self. The objective self is the person as he is for others—i.e., the economic, social, cultural and political roles he plays. The subjective self is the person as he experiences his actions and the events surrounding those actions. Hence the notion of self-interest in utilitarian explanation is conceptually straightforward, while the notion of self-interest in functionalist explanation is not. Indeed, in marxist theory the distinction is sometimes made between self-interests (corresponding to what a person experiences as being of benefit) and real interests (corresponding to what the person's interests ought to be given the social roles he occupies).

John Maguire argues that Marx's conception of politics was based primarily on this notion of the divided self, rather than politics based on class as such.

> The simple account correlates politics with class, and claims that the state will normally be a servant of the owning class. . . . The complex [alienation-based] account recognizes that precisely because of the 'unplanned' and 'unmanageable' nature of divided society, the owning class can find itself in a situation where the conflict with the working class requires that the state—the 'insurance company'—be given power not only over the individual owning-class members, but over the owning class as such, as the only way of meeting the political challenge of the subject class.[43]

In practice, this means that legislators, bureaucrats, scientists and citizen activists act in the way that they do for two kinds of reasons. They take actions because of personal motivations and desires (i.e., utility functions). They also take actions because of what counts as being a good scientist, a skillful legislator, an effective bureaucrat or a responsible citizen.

SUMMARY AND CONCLUSION

The field of environmental economics is dominated by neoclassical analysis. The political economics of these analyses focuses on the supply of and demand for environmental quality. This chapter veered away dramatically from this approach, concluding with a rather abstract discussion of three-dimensional power. The final section on hegemony is intended to elucidate the concept of the third dimension of power: the consensual exclusion of alternatives, preferential treatment of alternatives, the deferential treatment of selected participants and their interests, and the derisive treatment of other participants and their interests.

In principle the first and second dimensions of power are compatible with some form of supply-and-demand model. The model would consist of a dynamic equilibrium where people apply resources available to them based on the trade-offs in costs and benefits for a particular public choice. Those with more resources *ceteris paribus* are therefore advantaged over those with fewer when a direct conflict of interest arises over the supply of a public good. It is an easy extrapolation from this first dimension of power to the case where the rules for decisionmaking (i.e., the second dimension of power) are themselves the objects of public choice.

The discussion of hegemony is intended to distinguish the third dimension of power as clearly as possible from the utilitarian model. The effect of hegemony may appear to be subjective—false consciousness as a psychological state in which desires are somehow the wrong ones. As a consequence, it might seem that the third dimension of power could be accommodated to a utilitarian model with hegemonic arguments in utility functions. Such a utility function would describe a person's willingness to pursue particular goals based on her preferences for things consumed, such as the desire for a brand of car, and for things of a higher order, such as the desire for professional esteem.

However, the trade-offs so central to the utilitarian analysis do not fit a three dimensional model of power. Trade-offs only make sense at the same level of interests. Standards of role fulfillment are not appropriately traded off against the consumption of goods. The desire for a car can be balanced against the desire for a vacation. But the desire for professional esteem cannot be balanced off against the desire for a car, vacation or any other good. The desire for professional esteem may be appropriately balanced against, for example, the desire for income. And income in this context means more than the general ability to purchase cars and vacations, but is instead an ability to pursue a particular social status.

Professional esteem, income status and similar do not depend on desire and money. Rather, they depend on how successfully a person meets the expectations of others and the material requirements for fulfilling social roles. A capitalist who does not want to make profits and who consequently succeeds in her goal is not a capitalist.

Hegemonic power explains how superstructural institutions function to preserve fundamental economic relations by showing how institutional roles create the appropriate expectations and material requirements. These expectations and material requirements required for role fulfillment prevent issues such as the environmental quality from abating the domination of the owning class over the means of production. The functionalist model states that institutions function to provide cohesion to the owning class and to maintain stable social relations. The implication of this hypothesis is that institutional change in environmental control has as its purpose stability in the mode of production, not change in environmental quality.

NOTES

1. Soja, Morales and Wolff [1983].

2. Steven Kelman [1981] makes this observation, along with an insightful analysis of the normative assumption buried in the putatively analytic and neutral policy recommendations of mainstream environmental economists. For the literature, see Fisher [1981].

3. More so with marxist economics than with institutional economics. Swaney [1988] provides an institutionalist approach, Sandbach [1980] a marxist approach.

4. Bernstein [1955] gave currency to the idea in the public administration literature. See Anthony Downs [1967] for a neoclassical economist's version in the vein of his *An Economic Theory Of Democracy* [1957], and elaborated with specific regard to environmental issues in "Up and down with ecology--the 'issue-attention cycle'" [1972]. A general literature review is found in Mitnick [1980].

5. Doty [1978].

6. Posner [1974].

7. In political science there is a similar tripartite division of traditions. See Whitt [1982] and Alford [1985] and [1975].

8. As a sampling of the diversity among neoclassical economists see Mueller [1989] and [1979], Jackson [1983], Stigler [1975], and Sproule-Jones [1982].

9. See Tool [1988], Tool and Samuels [1989] and Stone [1982].

10.   Some in the Marxist tradition may not subscribe entirely to the Marxist theory of historical development (i.e., historical materialism), but nonetheless adopt the dynamics Marxist class analysis--i.e., where "elite" and "economic elite" are synonymous with "capitalist class." See Hoffman [1988], Miliband [1989], Cohen [1988] and [1978] and Jessop [1983].

11.   Miliband [1989]. See also the articles by Miliband [1968:3-11], Sweezy [1968:113-132] and Aptheker [1968:133-164].

12.   Maguire [1978 : 227].

13.   Garfinkel [1981:21].

14.   Jackson [1983]; Mueller [1989] and [1979]; Posner [1974].

15.   Baumol and Oates [1975].

16.   Baumol and Oates [1975:211].

17.   Goldberg [1974 : 461].

18.   Cohen [1978 : 35-36] and [1974 : 90-96].

19.   Cohen [1978 : Chapter 3]. For example, Cohen begins the chapter by saying

        The economic structure of a society is the whole set of its production relations. Production relations are relations of effective power over persons and productive forces, not relations of legal ownership. Cohen [1978 : 63].

20.   Except insofar as they act as the agent of (i.e., in the interest of) the owners of the means of production for whom they work.

21.   Miliband [1989] has a more sophisticated partition of class structure, consisting of eight categories. The basic differences used in the present study are valid in Miliband's. Moreover, this tripartite structure in roles does not imply a deviation from the

basic conception traditionally held by marxists that the constitutive conflict in capitalist society is between the owning class on the one hand, and the proletariat and other subordinate classes on the other. Cohen [1978 : 68-72].

22.　Cohen [1978 : 73-74].

23.　Baumol and Oates [1975:16-18].

24.　Kapp [1974] and [1971].

25.　Cohen [1988]; Dennett [1971].

26.　Lukes [1974]; Hoffman [1988].

27.　Domhoff [1979].

28.　Crenson [1971].

29.　Greer [1974].

30.　See Hoffman [1988] for a further discussion of Lukes' thesis.

31.　Hoffman [1988], Jessop [1983] and [1977]. This conflict became prominent in the English language literature most recently in an exchange between Ralph Miliband and Nicos Poulantzas in *The New Left Review* in the early 1970s, beginning with Poulantzas [1969] and continuing with Miliband [1973]. That particular debate had the field divided between 'instrumentalists' and 'structuralists'. Both Hoffman and Jessop summarize the debate.

32.　The concept of hegemony was first introduced into the marxist literature by Lenin and subsequently made into a dominant issue by Gramsci. Anderson [1977].

33.　Hoffman [1988]; Jessop [1983].

34.   Abercrombie, Hill and Turner [1980].

35.   Maguire [1978].

36.   Sen [1977] and Sen and Williams [1982].

37.   Maguire [1978] and Miliband [1983].

38.   Even in the mainstream, economists are calling for a broader interpretation of "interests." A.O. Hirschman has, for example, argued in favor of introducing a concept distinct from utility as a basis for describing rational action and for prescribing welfare improvements. Hirschman [1984]; see also Coleman [1984] who shared the symposium with Hirschman.

39.   Abercrombie, Hill and Turner [1980] and Abercrombie and Turner [1978]; Mann [1975] and [1970]; Connolly [1972]; Balbus [1971].

40.   Fischer [1979] and Ollman [1976].

41.   Cohen [1974]; Mann [1975] and [1970]; Maguire [1979].

42.   Hollis [1977 : Chapter 1].

43.   Maguire [1978 : 227-228].

REFERENCES

Abercrombie, Nicolas, Hill, Stephen and Turner, Bryan S. 1980. *The dominant ideology thesis*. London: Allen and Unwin.

Abercrombie, Nicolas and Turner, Bryan. 1978. The dominant ideology thesis. *British journal of sociology*. 29:2 (1978), 149-170.

Alford, Robert R., et al eds. 1975. *Stress and contradiction in modern capitalism*. Lexington, MA: D.C. Heath.

Alford, Robert R. 1975. Paradigms of relations between state and society. Alford, Robert R., et al. *Stress and contradiction in modern capitalism*. Lexington, MA: D.C. Heath. 145-160.

Alford, Robert R. and Friedland, Roger. 1985. *Powers of theory: capitalism, the state, and democracy*. Cambridge: New York.

Anderson, Perry. 1977. The antinomies of Antonio Gramsci. *New left review*. 100 (January, 1977), 5-78.

Aptheker, Herbert. 1968. Power in America. G. William Domhoff and Hoyt B. Ballard, eds. *C. Wright Mills and the power elite*. Boston: Beacon. 133-164.

Balbus, Isaac D. 1971. The concept of interest in pluralist and marxian analysis. *Politics and society*. 1:2 (February, 1971), 151-177.

Barton, Stephen E. 1983. Property rights and human rights: efficiency and democracy as criteria for regulatory reform. *Journal of economic issues*. 17:4 (December, 1983), 915-930.

Baumol, William J. 1969. *Welfare economics and the theory of the state*. Cambridge, MA: Harvard.

Baumol, William J. and Oates, Wallace E. 1975. *The theory of environmental policy: externalities, public outlays and the quality of life*. Englewood Cliffs, NJ:Prentice-Hall.

Bernstein, Marver H. 1955. *Regulating business by independent commission*. Princeton: Princeton University.

Brown, Alan. 1986. *Modern political philosophy: theories of the just society*. New York: Viking.

Capra, Fritjof. 1982. *The turning point: science, society, and the rising culture*. New York: Bantam.

Cohen, G.A. 1974. Being, consciousness and roles: on the foundations of historical materialism. Abramsky, C. ed. *Essays in honour of E.H. Carr*. London: Basil Blackwell. 83-97.

Cohen, G.A. 1978. *Marx's theory of history: a defence*. Princeton: Princeton University

Cohen, G.A. 1988. *History, labour, and freedom: themes from marx*. Clarendon: Oxford.

Coleman, James S. 1973. *The mathematics of collective action*. Chicago: Aldine.

Coleman, James S. 1980. Authority systems. *Public opinion quarterly*. (Summer, 1980), 143-162.

Coleman, James S. 1984. Introducing social structure into economic analysis. *American economic review, papers and proceedings*. 74:2 (May, 1984), 84-88.

Coleman. James S. 1973. Loss of power. *American sociological review*. 38:1 (February, 1973), 1-17.

Commoner, Barry. 1990. *Making peace with the planet*. New York: Pantheon.

Commoner, Barry. 1971. *The closing circle: nature, man and technology.* New York: Bantam.

Comstock, David. 1982. Power in organizations: toward a critical theory. *Pacific sociological review.* 25:2 (April, 1982), 139-162.

Connolly, William E. 1972. On 'interests' in politics. *Politics and society.* 2:3 (Summer, 1972), 459-477.

Crenson, Matthew A. 1971. *The unpolitics of air pollution: a study of nondecisionmaking in the cities.* Baltimore: Johns Hopkins University.

Dennett, Daniel. 1971. Intentional systems. *Journal of philosophy.* 68 (February, 1971), 87-106.

Dennett, Daniel. 1976. Conditions of personhood. Rorty, Amelie Oksenberg, ed. *The identities of persons.* Berkeley: University of California. 175-196.

Domhoff, G. William. 1979. *The powers that be: processes of ruling class domination in America.* New York: Vintage.

Domhoff, G. William and Ballard, Hoyt B. eds. 1968. *C. Wright Mills and the power elite.* Boston: Beacon.

Domhoff, G. William. 1970. *The higher circles: the governing class in America.* New York: Vintage.

Doty, Robert Adam. 1978. Life cycle theories of regulatory agency behavior: the Los Angeles Air Pollution Control District. Ph.D. Dissertation, University of California, Riverside.

Downs, Anthony. 1972. Up and down with ecology: the issue-attention cycle. *The public interest.* 28 (1972), 38-50.

Downs, Anthony. 1967. *Inside bureaucracy.* Boston: Little, Brown and Company.

Downs, Anthony. 1957. *An economic theory of democracy*. New York: Harper and Row.

Doyal, Len and Harris, Roger. 1983. The practical foundations of human understanding. *New left review*. 139 (June, 1983), 59-78.

Elster, Jon. 1982. Sour grapes: utilitarianism and the genesis of wants. Sen, Amartya and Williams, Bernard, eds. *Utilitarianism and beyond*. Cambridge: Cambridge University. 219-238.

Fischer, Norman. 1979. *Economy and self: philosophy and economics from the Mercantilists to Marx*. Westport, CN: Greenwood.

Fisher, Anthony C. 1981. *Resource and environmental economics*. Cambridge:Cambridge University.

Fox, Richard Wightman and Lears, T.J. Jackson eds. 1983. *The culture of consumption: critical essays in American history 1880-1980*. New York: Pantheon.

Garfinkel, Alan. 1981. *Forms of explanation: rethinking the questions in social theory*. New Haven: Yale University.

Goldberg, Victor P. 1974. Institutional change and the quasi-invisible hand. *Journal of law and economics*. 17:2 (1974), 461-496.

Goldberg, Victor P. 1982. Peltzman on regulation and politics. *Public choice*. 39 (1982), 291-297.

Goldman, Alvin. 1972. Toward a theory of social power. *Philosophical studies*. 23 (1972), 221-268.

Greer, Edward. 1974. Air pollution and corporate power: municipal reform limits in a black city. *Politics and society*. 4:4 (1974), 483-510.

Harvey, David. 1982. *The limits to capital*. Chicago: University of Chicago.

Hoffman, John. 1988. *States, power and democracy: contentious concepts in practical political theory.* New York: St. Martin's.

Hirschman, Albert O. 1984. Against parsimony: three easy ways of complicating some categories of economic analysis. *American economic review, papers and proceedings.* 74:2 (May, 1984), 88-96.

Hollis, Martin and Nell, Edward. 1975. *Rational economic man: a philosophical critique of neoclassical economics.* Cambridge: Cambridge University.

Hollis, Martin. 1977. *Models of man: philosophical thoughts on social action.* Cambridge: Cambridge University.

Holloway, John and Picciotto, Sol ed. 1978. *State and capital: a marxist debate.* Austin: University of Texas.

Jackson, P.M. 1983. *The political economy of bureaucracy.* New York: Barnes and Noble.

Jessop, Bob. 1983. *The capitalist state: marxist theories and methods.* New York: New York University.

Jessop, Bob. 1977. Recent theories of the capitalist state. *Cambridge journal of economics.* 1 (1977), 353-373.

Jessop, Bob. 1980. On recent marxist theories of law, the state, and juridico-political ideology. *International journal of the sociology of law.* 8 (1980), 339-368.

Kapp, K. William. 1974. *Environmental policies and development planning in contemporary China and other essays.* The Hague: Monton.

Kapp, K. William. 1971. *The social costs of private enterprise.* New York: Schocken.

Kelman, Steven. 1981. *What price incentives? economists and the environment.* Boston: Auburn House Publishing.

Leiss, William. 1979. *The limits to satisfaction: an essay on the problem of needs and commodities*. Toronto: University of Toronto.

Los Angeles *Times*. 1981. Air quality district accused of laxity. Part I (September 24, 1981), 1.

Lukes, Steven. 1974. *Power: a radical perspective*. Bristol: J.W. Arrowsmith.

Maguire, John. 1978. *Marx's theory of politics*. Cambridge: Cambridge University.

Maguire, John. 1979. Contract, coercion and consciousness. Harrison, Ross, *Rational action*. Cambridge: Cambridge University Press. 157-173.

Mann, Michael. 1975. The ideology of intellectuals and other people in the development of capitalism. Alford, Robert R., et al, ed. *Stress and contradiction in modern capitalism*. Lexington, MA: D.C. Heath. 275-308.

Mann, Michael. 1970. The social cohesion of liberal democracy. *American sociological review*. 35 (1970), 423-439.

Marsden, Peter V. 1983. Restricted access in networks and models of power. *American journal of sociology*. 88:4 (1983), 686-717.

Marshall, Gordon. 1983. Some remarks on the study of working class consciousness. *Politics and society*. 12:13 (1983), 263-301.

McLellan, David. 1979. *Marxism after Marx: an introduction*. Boston: Houghton Mifflin.

McLellan, David. 1986. *Ideology*. Minneapolis, MN: University of Minnesota.

Miliband, Ralph. 1989. *Divided societies: class struggle in contemporary capitalism*. Clarendon: Oxford.

Miliband, Ralph. 1983. State power and class interests. *New left review.* 138 (April, 1983), 57-68.

Miliband, Ralph. 1973. Poulantzas and the capitalist state. *New left review.* 82 (December, 1973), 83-92.

Miliband, Ralph. 1968. C. Wright Mills. G. William Domhoff and Hoyt B. Ballard, eds. *C. Wright Mills and the power elite.* Boston: Beacon. 3-11.

Mitnick, Barry M. 1980. *The political economy of regulation.* New York: Columbia University.

Mueller, Dennis C. 1989. *Public choice II.* Cambridge: Cambridge University.

Mueller, Dennis C. 1979. *Public choice.* Cambridge: Cambridge University.

Ollman, Bertell. 1976. *Alienation: Marx's conception of man in capitalist society.* Cambridge: Cambridge University.

Posner, Richard A. 1974. Theories of economic regulation. *The Bell journal of economics and management science.* 5:2 (Autumn, 1974), 335-358.

Poulantzas, Nicos. 1969. The problem of the capitalist state. *New left review.* 58 (December, 1969), 67-78.

Samuels, Warren and Shaffer, James. 1982. Deregulation: the principle inconclusive arguments. *Policy studies review.* 1:3 (1982), 463-469.

Sandbach, Francis. 1982. *Principles of pollution control.* London: Longman.

Sandbach, Francis. 1980. *Environment, ideology and policy.* Montclair, NJ: Allanheld, Osmun and Company.

Schmidt, Alfred. 1971. *The concept of nature in Marx.* London: New Left Books.

Sen, Amartya K. 1977. Rational fools: a critique of the behavioral foundations of economic theory. *Philosophy and public affairs.* 6 (1977), 31-74.

Sen, Amartya K. 1970. The impossibility of a paretian liberal. *Journal of political economy.* 78 (1970), 152-157.

Sen, Amartya and Williams, Bernard eds. 1982. *Utilitarianism and beyond.* Cambridge: Cambridge University.

Sennett, Richard. 1976. *The fall of public man: on the social psychology of capitalism.* New York: Vintage.

Shaw, William H. 1978. *Marx's theory of history.* Stanford: Stanford University.

Soja, Edward, Morales, Rebecca and Wolff, Goetz. 1983. Urban restructuring: an analysis of social and spatial change in Los Angeles. *Economic geography.* 59:2 (April, 1983), 195-230.

Sproule-Jones, Mark. 1982. Public choice and natural resources: methodological explication and critique. *The American political science review.* 76 (1982), 790-803.

Stigler, George J. 1975. *The citizen and the state: essays on regulation.* Chicago: University of Chicago.

Stone, Alan. 1982. *Regulation and its alternatives.* Washington, DC: Congressional Quarterly.

Sweezy, Paul M. 1968. Power elite or ruling class?. G. William Domhoff and Hoyt B. Ballard, eds. *C. Wright Mills and the power elite.* Boston: Beacon. 115-132.

Tool, Marc R., ed. 1988. *Evolutionary economics.* Vols. I and II. Armonk, NY: M.E. Sharpe.

Tool, Marc R. and Samuels, Warren J. 1989. *The economy as a system of power.* New Brunswick, NJ: Transaction Publishers.

Whitt, J. Allen. 1982. *Urban elites and mass transportation: the dialectics of power.* Princeton: Princeton University.

Worster, Donald. 1979. *Nature's economy: the roots of ecology.* Garden City, NY: Anchor/Doubleday.

Wright, Erik Olin. 1978. *Class, crisis and the state.* London: New Left Books.

CHAPTER 2

Environmental Politics

"We looked pretty bad," Joseph "Jeb" Stuart told a reporter.

"They had the cards stacked against us. . . . It isn't that we haven't been trying."[1]

Mr. Stuart made his remarks in response to hearings held before the California State Assembly Committee on Energy and Natural Resources at the University of California, Los Angeles on September 22 and 23, 1981. When he made these statements Jeb Stuart was the Executive Officer of the South Coast Air Quality Management District.[2] This multi-county district (and its predecessor County Air Pollution Control Districts) has the longest continuous history of modern air pollution regulation in California and the United States. The Assembly Committee was reviewing the past performance of the District (generally referred to by its acronym SCAQMD) in order to evaluate the desirability of changes in the structure of SCAQMD. A Committee Staff background paper informed Committee members that the "two issues which will be examined are the potential for improving the enforcement of air quality regulations and the need for increasing the public accountability of the South Coast Board [of Directors] and citizen participation in District operations."[3]

These issues had been raised because of criticisms directed at the District by two groups: environmental activists and the California Air Resources Board (CARB).[4] A reporter for the Riverside, California *Press-Enterprise* characterized the criticisms made at the hearings by saying that "most of the arguments are not new and were made by people locked in long-standing controversy with the District and its policies."[5] Thomas Heinsheimer, then Chairman of SCAQMD's Board of Directors, characterized the criticisms of the District as coming "from people eager to hold the District up to embarrassment and ridicule."[6]

The criticisms made by CARB, which were delivered at the hearings by its Chair, Mary Nichols, focused on the enforcement program of SCAQMD. The source document for her criticisms was a study of the major County Air Pollution Control District enforcement programs in California issued in late August, 1981 by CARB.[7] The study was the result of directions placed in the Air Resources Board's budget by Mel Levine, at the time a West Los Angeles assemblyperson[8] and member of the Committee On Energy And Natural Resources.[9]

In her testimony at the UCLA hearings, Ms. Nichols contrasted SCAQMD with the other Districts included in the CARB study, most notably the San Diego County Air Pollution Control District and the San Francisco Bay Area Air Quality Management District. The contrast presented by Ms. Nichols portrayed SCAQMD as undermotivated in the enforcement of its regulations. First, annual testing of major sources for regulatory compliance were inadequate (although acknowledged to be improving). Second, the majority of tests actually conducted were conducted with the prior knowledge of the sources (whereas in the Bay Area District 65% of the tests were unannounced). And third, the SCAQMD had a relative paucity of inspectors for major sources (7.3 sources per inspector for the SCAQMD compared to 4.9 sources per inspector for the Bay Area District).[10]

Ms. Nichols' testimony was seconded by Ira Reiner, the newly elected District Attorney for the City of Los Angeles.[11] Mr. Reiner went so far as to ask the Committee for legislative relief for the City of Los Angeles so that his office could seek more vigorously than SCAQMD improvements in "the level of industry compliance with . . . regulations through the prosecution and assessment of civil penalties."[12]

Early in the hearing Jan Chattan-Brown, an Orange County attorney who had represented several litigants against SCAQMD, related her experience and concluded that the "basic policy of the District is to obtain industry's co-operation, rather than aggressively enforce rules."[13]

Mr. Heinsheimer responded to this criticism of the District's enforcement efforts by saying that "there is no evidence that the total emissions in the [South Coast Air] Basin are being worsened by massive industrial non-compliance."[14]   In response to questions about the imposition of fees charged to non-complying sources, Mr. Stuart said that "we [SCAQMD] feel we have some responsibility not to go overboard." Mr. Levine summarized his impression of the District's testimony on this enforcement facet of the hearings by saying that "what you're suggesting to me is that non-compliance is something you don't care very much about."[15]

The other major criticism of the District concerned the structure of decisionmaking: the way in which enforcement and other policies were formed and by whom. Representing the environmental group Clean Air Now, Judy Orttung[16] pointed out that no member of SCAQMD's Board of Directors lived in the smoggiest parts of the District. In fact, she noted, three members of the Board lived entirely outside the District itself. These facts were alluded to by Ms. Orttung not so much as central issues but as indicative of more crucial problems in the way the District dedicated itself to the abatement of air pollution and the resolve with which it pursued this goal. More fundamental from her perspective was the fact that the District was not implementing its own policies as these were specified in SCAQMD's Air Quality Management Plan: only 13 of the 35 measures specified in this 1979 Plan had been implemented by 1981.

Ms. Orttung's conclusion was that the District Board had arrogated to itself policy-making powers not delegated to it by the State legislation when the District was created in 1977. She therefore recommended that selection of District Board members be radically changed in order to increase their political accountability. In addition, Ms. Orttung recommended that an ombudsman-like Office of Public Adviser be created within the District to facilitate citizen access to the decisionmaking processes and operations of the District.[17]

Following Ms. Orttung, Gladys Meade presented her views to the Committee. Ms. Meade was at the time the "public" member of the District Board, having been appointed by Governor Edmond G. Brown, Jr. After reviewing the legislative mandate and record of the Board of Directors of SCAQMD, Ms. Meade observed that "we [the Board of Directors] are not adopting the most stringent rules and regulations or employing the best administrative and management practices. . . . Why?

There appears to be an institutionalized bias against adopting a rule or regulation that is opposed by industry or proposed as a 'model rule' by the Air Resources Board . . . or if there is perceived support for the regulation by an environmental or citizens' group. This bias is exercised even if the staff recommendation is a favorable one. Added to this is a pervasive fortress mentality that assumes assault from other agencies is either occurring or is imminent. These assaults are repulsed in two ways: first, by counter-attack on a personal basis with cries of 'deliberate attempts to misrepresent' and 'impugns the South Coast District' . . . [followed] by a flood of technical information which challenges the smallest and most insignificant point raised by the identified opposition. If the skirmish is not won on the data or if exhaustion has not overtaken all involved in the debate, then the fallback position is doubt-mongering so that the burden of uncertainty grows to immense proportions."[18]

As a consequence of these hearings, one year later the California Assembly passed legislation that changed the structure of the Board of Directors of the South Coast Air Quality Management District: the number of Board members was increased from 10 to 14; all Board members would now be required to reside within the District; greater representation was given to Orange, San Bernardino and Riverside Counties[19]; and two additional "public" members were to be appointed.[20]

THE CHARACTERISTICS OF ENVIRONMENTAL POLITICS

The preceding vignette captures the four characteristics of environmental politics: citizen activism; a seemingly unresponsive bureaucracy; normative conflict; and exfoliation.

Individuals such as Judy Orttung are typical of environmental activists and their role in the growth of the environmental institutions. Individuals such as Jeb Stuart are characteristic of the professionals who implement the environmental policies created by legislative bodies.

Assemblyman Levine's observation regarding the dedication of the SCAQMD's enforcement activity and Board member Heinscheimer's response are typical of the range of norms in conflict over the seriousness of air pollution.   And Gladys Meade's criticism of SCAQMD's use of its technical expertise as a defensive mechanism demonstrates how the science of air pollution emerges or exfoliates as regulatory efforts themselves develop.

In "The Structure Of Environmental Politics Since World War II,"[21] Samuel P. Hays discusses the first two important characteristics of Post-War environmental politics. First, he notes that the impetus for environmental regulation and reform has for the most part come from the activism of people at the community level—those people who are immediately affected by environmental degradation. Second, he notes that this activism is directed against what are perceived to be public organizations whose nominal purpose is specifically the prevention of the environmental degradation or generally the protection of the citizen's interests.

In an early set of studies, Lynton Caldwell, Lynton Hayes and Isabel MacWhirter affirmed both of these features of environmental politics in a series of case studies among a broad range of environmental issues.[22] In over 70 case studies, Caldwell, Hayes and MacWhirter observed the "grass roots" phenomenon of citizen activism, formalizing it in the concept "Functional Citizenship." Caldwell, Hayes and MacWhirter define this concept in terms of participation in public decisionmaking. The functional citizen acts out of a desire to see implemented what they regard as the public interest. Another author describes this kind of activity as "lobbying for the people": people taking actions intended to improve the delivery of an item of collective consumption, where achieving the goal will not selectively benefit them.[23]

Later studies of this phenomenon, such as *Habits of the Heart*[24], stress the quasi-altruistic nature of such activities. Hays, however, has focused on more conservative motives, namely the preservation of the quality of life at the community level.[25] Hays and others also point up the less romantic role played by a rising standard of living and the time and income that afford the appreciation and enjoyment of environmental goods.[26] Even an even wider array of motives can be assayed to account for the fact of environmental activism[27], but the fact of its prominence is indisputable.

The second characteristic, that of the prominent role played by the managerial structures in impeding abatement of environmental degradation, is reinforced by Caldwell, Hayes and MacWhirter when they observe that

> a pattern or characteristic sequence of events appeared that the authors and editor had not foreseen.[28]

> The cases reported . . . repeatedly illustrate the conviction of public and business administrators that they represent the public interest. . . . The acrimony characterizing many environmental disputes reflects moral indignation felt on both sides of the controversy. The environmentally concerned citizen sees the public or business official as sacrificing or betraying the interest of society at large for some special economic or political purpose that is substantially or morally wrong whatever its legality. The officials see the protestors as self-appointed troublemakers interfering with the orderly, lawful, and efficient processes of government or business.[29]

These two aspects of environmental politics are interrelated. According to Caldwell, Hayes and MacWhirter, reforms appropriate to this interrelationship require the reconciliation of "Functional Citizenship" with the need for technically accurate and achievable policies.

> The fact that citizens have repeatedly been compelled to organize to defend the environment against the agencies of government is a truth, but it is not all of the truth concerning the politics of environmental quality in the United States. That voluntary citizen action has been a positive and constructive force for more responsible government is, however, a generalization that we believe will stand without successful challenge.[30]

The picture painted by such studies is that environmental politics develop from a fundamental conflict of interest between citizens and public bureaucracies. Central to the conflict is the frequent need for 'consumers' of environmental services to press their interests. The two-dimensional view of power works here.

For those on the outside, the institutions responsible for making environmental improvements consistently perform inadequately. They not only fail to do their job[31] but seem to actively thwart the will of what would appear to be the institution's natural constituency. The problem, of course, is that environmental control agencies have more than environmental activists as their constituencies.

A picture of the regulatory process is given by Paul Downing and is reproduced on the next page in Figure 2-1. This diagram displays the complexity of the regulatory process, especially in distinguishing among agency action, court action and the budgetary process. Another interesting feature of the diagram is its explicit acknowledgement of the bargaining process that goes on between the agency and other actors: polluters, courts, legislators, the polluted and environmental activists.

There are two curious features to the picture. First, the physical phenomenon of environmental quality is literally peripheral to the process. In fact, it appears nowhere in the regulator's universe—for instance, in meeting standards as a legislative mandate. The second curious feature is that the driving force behind the regulators action is the budget. This has to do with marginalist economist attempt to lock onto what motivates the regulator, with the answer being the size of his budget.[32] However, as Hays work has shown, the size of an agency's budget has less to do with its effectiveness than the willingness of its personnel to enforce the pertinent legislation.

The willingness to act, and the administrative latitude that allows for degrees of enforcement, is a much richer phenomenon than the size of a budget. Although the quantity of resources available is important, it is not so critical as their deployment. And the most salient feature of the administrative politics that determines how the regulatory budget is deployed is the role that regulators see themselves as fulfilling.

The attitude exhibited specifically by Jeb Stuart and more generally by the environmental regulators discussed by Hays and Caldwell is rather technocratic. Smog is a technically complex problem than should be left to the experts. Moreover, the environmental agency is not intended to be an institution for environmental advocacy but an institution for environmental improvement. The responsible approach, as Jeb Stuart and Thomas Heinscheimer indicated, is to improve environmental quality in balance with other social goals.

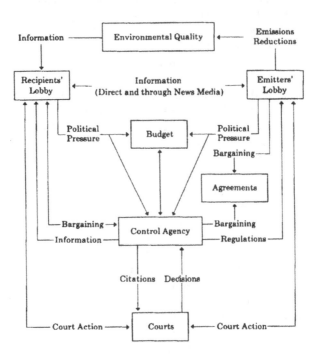

Figure 2-1
The flow of environmental regulation (Downing [1984:128])

This situation is reinforced for air pollution control in California because local politicians (technically "legislators" in Downing's diagram) sit as governing boards for air pollution agencies. The South Coast Air Quality Management District, for instance, can be viewed either as the local politicians who sit as the Board of Directors of the District or as the administrative, technical and bureaucratic personnel of the District. The local politicians implement state and federal policy and respond to various forms of lobbying activity on the part of citizen activists and business interests. It is the administrative, technical and bureaucratic personnel who implement the policies established by the local politicians.[33]

This basic structural conflict between the role that citizen activists expect regulators to play and the role regulators see themselves playing manifests itself in other ways. The most apparent is the way in which various participants in environmental politics define the problem itself. The less apparent way is in how the science of environmental regulation emerges from the practice of environmental regulation itself.

In January, 1982 Carl Builder and Morlie Graubard of the RAND Corporation completed a study for SCAQMD. The District had commissioned the study to help in restructuring its internal organization and was a direct consequence of the hearing reported above. In the Final Report[34]--*A Conceptual Approach To Strategies For The Control Of Air Pollution In The South Coast Air Basin*--Builder and Graubard identify three different views of the air pollution problem in Southern California. Each view was held by people who were both knowledgeable and actively involved with the issue. The three views, as articulated by Builder and Graubard, are that:

Air pollution is a public nuisance (causing disamenities, inconveniences and short-term debilitation to a small, sensitive portion of the population);

Air pollution is a health hazard (causing chronic debilities and permanent impairment of health); and

Air pollution is a danger (causing death during severe episodes and in the long-run causing increased mortality due to the increased exposure to mutagens and carcinogens).[35]

Within this framework, Builder and Graubard clearly identify SCAQMD as institutionally holding to the 'public nuisance' view of Southern California's air pollution problems. Moreover, this is the view that air pollution regulators in Southern California have consistently taken.

On the other hand, the 'grassroots' activists who have historically called for improvements in air pollution regulation in Southern California have moved from a 'public nuisance' view to a 'hazard/danger' view. This shift took place in conjunction with an increase in two things: knowledge about the effects of air pollution and an understanding that the scope of the problem was much broader than originally defined.[36]

Encouraging environmental activism has not been a favored strategy among air pollution regulators. The dominant mode of management activity among a very broad range of environmental regulators in Southern California and across the United States has been a kind of constructive engagement.[37] The dominant view held by air pollution engineers (who comprise the bulk of the regulatory bureaucracy) is that air pollution is inefficient. Businesses should therefore not be penalized so much as educated about the waste represented by air pollution.

This approach to the problem of air pollution is not accidental. Mechanical engineers as a profession have dominated the air pollution control profession for much of its history. This professional group has an identifiable ideology which has promoted the self-conception of mechanical engineers as the mid-wives of a neutral technological progress within the context of corporate capitalism.[38]

What this emphasizes is not simply that people disagree on how serious a problem air pollution is, but that the disagreement is ideologically based. There are two things at work here. On the one hand, there may be disagreements over the factual basis for defining air pollution as a nuisance, danger or hazard. On the other hand, the disagreement may be more fundamental: even though evidence may not be contentious, the *relative* importance of air pollution compared to, for instance, a "healthy economy" (i.e., public and private institutions and policies that promote growth) may be in serious dispute. This latter is in fact the practical side of Garfinkel's conception of an explanatory space—e.g., is a little smog all that hazardous compared to insecure employment possibilities. The difficult aspect of this normative conflict is that it appears not primarily as a conflict of values but as a conflict over the facts. This blends into the final feature of environmental politics: exfoliation.

Early efforts by activists depended heavily on the knowledge of the regulatory agency itself. Factually, the agency and activists held the same view of the technical problems involved. But with increasing technical sophistication and independence bred by a growing failure of confidence in the regulatory agencies, activist and many professionals outside SCAQMD took issue with the facts that supported the actions of the District.

One of the distinguishing characteristics of the environmental issues that have emerged since the end of World War II is the technical complexity of the underlying problems. And not only technical complexity (a feature shared by many institutions and activities that have come under regulatory control), but a protean nature as well—environmental problems virtually always seem to become more intractable and the effects turn out to be even more pervasive and lethal as social institutions attempt to manage them.

The fourth and final feature of environmental politics is described in yet another study that has smog in Southern California as its subject. In their study of motor vehicle air pollution control, James Krier and Edmund Ursin observed that the technically complex process of discovering the physical causes of air pollution were intimately bound up with the policy formation and implementation process.

What is more interesting, however, is the manner in which policy unconsciously produced *unsystematic* knowledge. It did so by a process of gradually exposing, layer by layer, inappropriate or insufficient responses to the pollution problem, at each stage arriving at a better understanding of what to do next. By the very steps it took, policy tended to ensure the existence of conditions that would themselves suggest the shortcomings of past steps and the directions for future ones. This process of "exfoliation" was a product of all of the considerations examined earlier . . . —inertia, uncertainty, crisis, fixations, and the whole pattern of policy-by-least-steps down the path of least resistance itself.[39]

[We] avoid the familiar phrase "trial and error" because it connotes an open acknowledgement of not knowing what to do and a consciously systematic experimental approach to finding out. Prior to 1970[40], policymakers generally believed they knew what to do (even if it was just to "find out" through *research*), and in any event almost never regarded their actions (other than those aimed at research) as experiments designed to produce knowledge. Yet those actions, by stripping away layers of misconceptions, uncertainties, and so forth—hence the label "exfoliation"—produced more knowledge than did research, or at least as much.[41]

This fourth feature is like the last in that it has two aspects. One aspect is straightforward: environmental degradations, as they have emerged since World War II, have required and stimulated genuine scientific discovery just to find out what sort of things social institutions were dealing with. Frequently, these investigations opened Pandora's box, producing a discovery of more than anyone really wanted to know or was prepared to handle. The other aspect has to do with what may be appropriately called the politics of science. The myth of pure science aside, the need for science-based policy brings to the foreground the important role of scientists and science-based professionals in policymaking. Part of the politics of science in environmental politics is the attempt to maintain that scientists can and should maintain a dispassionate distance from the social effects of policymaking and implementation.

Such neutrality has been problematic at best in the South Coast Air Basin. But fact mongering is not unique to smog in Southern California.[42] Moved by what they perceived to be the unresponsiveness of the institutions of environmental improvement, citizen activists have felt compelled to become technical experts in their own right. As their alarm grew with the discovery of an ever bleaker picture of deteriorating environmental quality, regulators and activists conflict even more—not simply over the willingness of the agency to act but over its basic understanding of and commitment to the environmental problem. And as these amalgams of factual and normative conflicts came to the fore, basic knowledge of the environmental problem was developed—not to solve the problem but to resolve an institutional conflict.

THE SUPPLY AND DEMAND FOR CLEAN AIR

The utilitarian model promotes the virtue of markets. That virtue rests on individual choice: the decision to purchase and the decision to consume are simultaneous. The problem with bureaucracies is that this virtue is distorted and even perverted. In public forums the decision to purchase and consume are not simultaneous. The people who decide on the quantity to consume of a public good are only a vanishing small portion of those who will consume that good. In collective consumption, there is at best only an indirect relationship between the enjoyment of the benefits of possessing a public good and the costs required to obtain that good.

This distance between decisionmakers and consumers is aggravated when decisionmaking takes place within bureaucracies. Legislative decisionmaking has the direct if tenuous feedback mechanism of periodic voting. Bureaucrats generally have no such direct feedback mechanism imposed on them. The self-interested regulator who is responsible for the delivery of environmental services chooses that level of delivery which maximizes her own career, income and consumption preferences.[43]

However, the regulator is more than an income maximizer. The regulator also has a set of professional norms to abide by, norms which define her self-consciousness toward environmental degradation. Without such a concept, the preference of the regulator would be to do nothing and collect a check. Instead, what is observed is the regulator not doing enough or doing the wrong things. This suggests that the confluence of professional norms and political pressures work to move the regulator to act as she does.

Figure 2-2 represents the willingness of the regulator to act. The vertical axis, labelled "Total WTA" for total willingness to act, measures the desirability of a course of action. The horizontal axis is labelled "Management Activity", which indicates a spectrum of intensity with which a regulator implements a policy, enforces a regulation or administrative rule, and so on. More than simple motion is measured along this axis, where 8 hours of the right kind of activity may have a greater management activity value than 40 hours of some other kind of activity. "Management Activity" is intended to capture Hays conception

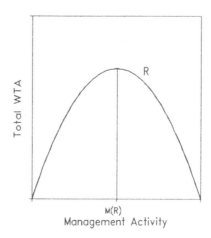

Figure 2-2

The willingness of regulators to take actions that improve environmental quality

of administrators as having considerable discretion in implementing and enforcing environmental policy.[44] The function **R** represents the interplay of professional norms with real politics. *M(R)* represents the intensity of action that the regulator regards as most desirable—for example, the pursuit of cooperation by polluters in enforcing an effluent standard rather than confrontation with them in court. *M(R)* is the best level of management activity. Management activity that is more intense (.e.g, litigation) is less desirable as is management activity the is less intense (e.g., ignoring violations altogether). *M(R)* represents the professionally responsible course of action. *M(R)* also formalizes the view held by regulators that environmentalists want too much and polluters want too little intervention.

Figure 2-3 shows the marginal willingness of regulators to take a particular course of action. The function **R'** is positive for management activity less vigorous than *M(R)* and is negative for management activity more vigorous than *M(R)*. When engaged in activities less than *M(R)*, the regulator will want to do more because each increment of activity

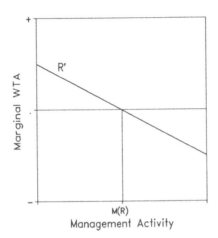

Figure 2-3
The marginal willingness of regulators to take actions that improve environmental
quality

that brings the management activity closer to *M(R)* brings more
satisfaction to the regulator. In the other direction, at greater levels of
management activity the regulator wants to act less aggressively because
a reduction in the severity of the action descreases the dissatisfaction
of the regulator.

But the regulator has more to deal with than her own
satisfaction—venal, professional or other. Two basic demands are made
on the regulator—do less or do more. At any given level of management
activity, each group will be willing to act so as to influence the
regulator. Environmentalists desiring a more aggressive level of
management activity may, for example, bring suit against the regulator
agency. Industrial polluters desiring less aggressive environmental
management may, for example, challenge the scientific and technical
assumptions behind the regulator's actions. The net offect of the
activities of environmentalists, polluters and others lining up for either

more or less environmental management is a cost imposed on the regulator.

The regulator faces a set of costs externally imposed, costs in the

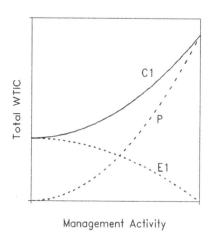

Figure 2-4

The willingness of "polluters" and "environmentalists" to impose costs on regulators

form of legal actions, public relations activities, public hearings and other activities required to fulfill the charter of the public agency. Figure 2-4 represents the cost function imposed on the regulator. The cost function C1 measures the net effect of two forces—those whose willingness to impose costs on the regulator increases with each level of management activity (P) and those whose willingness decreases as management intensity increases (E1). At low levels of management, environmentalists are enraged and are willing to impose considerable costs while polluters have no incentive to act. Conversely, at high levels of management polluters have a great willingness to impose costs on the regulator, while environmentalists have no incentive to act.[45]

C1 is the total willingness to impose costs (WTIC) at each level of management activity by both polluters and environmentalists, vertically summing the functions P and E1. The regulator must balance these

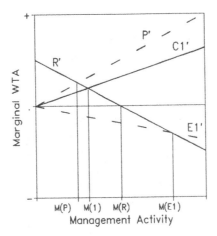

Figure 2-5
The equilibrium level of management activity

costs against her own willingness to act in support of implementing environmental policies. Figure 2-5 shows the marginal willingness to impose costs on the regulator by environmentalists and polluters (the function **C1'**) on the marginal willingness to act by the regulator (the function **R'**). The intersection of these two functions yields the equilibrium level of management *M(1)*. At management levels greater than *M(1)*, for instance at the regulator's ideal level *M(R)*, polluters are willing to impose additional costs greater than the willingness of the regulator to sustain that level of management. At levels less than *M(1)*, the regulator has a willingness to act aggressively that is greater than the willingness of interest groups to impose costs.

Two other functions and corresponding equilibria appear in the figure. The function **P'** represents the polluter's marginal willingness to impose costs. The intersection of **P'** with **R'** at *M(P)* represents the "right" outcome so far as those desiring less aggressive management are concerned. Likewise, the function **E1'** represents the environmentalist's marginal willingness to impose costs. The intersection of **E1'** with **R'** at $M(E1)$ represents the "right" outcome from the perspective of those desiring more aggressive environmental management.

In comparison with the regulator's desired level of management activity, polluters will systematically appear to want less management while environmentalists will systematically appear to want more. The equilibrium level of management at $M(1)$ is not a happy outcome for anyone—too much for polluters, too little for regulators and scandalously too little for environmentalists.

The outcome in Figure 2-5 is only one possibility. As it so happens, it is the common outcome. Environmental agencies do less than the regulators think they could, but not excessively so. Polluters think that the management activities of the agency are excessive but not onerous. And environmentalist view the regulator and polluter as having essentially identical positions. In contrast, polluters and regulators view environmentalists as uncompromising radicals.

But other outcomes are possible. For example, a vast upwelling of environmentalist sentiment could cause a substantial shift upward in the function describing the environmentalist's willingness to impose costs on regulators. That is, an upward shift in the function **E1** in Figure 2-4, so that the net willingness to impose cost function shifts from the upward sloping **C1** to a downward sloping **C2** (not shown). Figure 2-6 shows the corresponding function **C2'** imposed on the regulator's marginal willingness to act function **R'**. The new equilibrium level of management is shown at $M(2)$. The old cost function **C1'** and corresponding equilibrium $M(1)$ are also shown.

The function **C1'** represents the ability of polluters to prevail in environmental politics. At each level of management, polluters have a greater marginal willingness to impose costs on regulators than environmentalists. Conversely, the function **C2'** represents the greater marginal willingness of environmentalists to impose costs than polluters. In such circumstances, regulators are forced to do more than they think is professionally proper.[46]

These relationships of the functions **R**, **P** and **E** capture the four features of environmental politics in a utilitarian model. This model further allows for a representation of structural change in environmental management. Citizen activism is represented most obviously in the function **E**, with structural change represented by shifts such as that discussed above from **C1** to **C2**. The role of regulators as seemingly unresponsive is represented by the function **R**. Normative

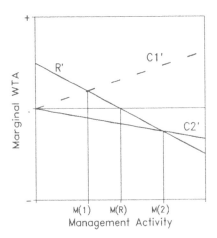

Figure 2-6
New equilibrium level of management activity due to increased importance of
environmental quality issues

conflict is represented by each of the three functions—from an equilibrium management level, polluters will always want less, environmentalists will always want more and regulators will want either more or less depending on where the balance is struck.

Finally, exfoliation is properly, if not obviously, represented by the regulator's function **R**. As the science of environmental degradation unfolds, several things happen. For one, the nature of the problem becomes better specified. With that better specification, the tools of monitoring and control improve. The model developed above assumes that the regulator wants to perform in a professionally responsible way to improve environmental quality. Improved science provides improved tools to do so. Thus, with exfoliation comes increased effectiveness at each level of the regulator's willingness to act.

The final part of this supply-demand model is the relationship of management activity to environmental quality itself. Figure 2-7 shows the relationship between the level of management activity and the rate

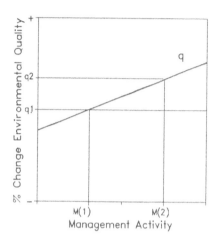

Figure 2-7
The relationship between management activity
and the rate of improvement in environmental quality

at which environmental quality improves. The assumption built into the
representation is that without any management activity, environmental
degradation occurs. With each increment in management activity,
environmental degradation is abated until environmental improvement
begins.

In Figure 2-7, the function **q** represents the relationship between
management activity and changes in environmental quality. The function
shows how regulatory activity affects the actual performance of
pollution sources. The effectiveness of policy instruments, or conversely,
the sensitivity of pollution sources to regulatory action is represented
by **q**.

The two management equilibria *M(1)* and *M(2)* are shown with
corresponding rates of environmental improvement, *q1* and *q2*. These
relationships are developed in Figure 2-8 into a hypothetical time series
of environmental quality data. The functional relationship is
linear—environmental quality changes by a given percentage each year.

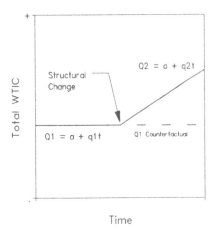

Figure 2-8

A hypothetical environmental quality time series showing structural change

What Figure 2-8 shows is a time series separated by structural change. Structural change occurs because the level of management activity has shifted from $M(1)$ to $M(2)$. Concomitantly, the function describing the level of environmental quality shifts from Q1 to Q2. A counterfactual is shown for the level of environmental quality had the structural change not occurred (i.e., the dashed line labelled "Q1 Counterfactual").

It is this basic model which is used in Chapters 4, 5 and 6 to determine whether institutional change in air quality management has occurred in Southern California. The Table 2-I below provides a brief summary of the model developed in this section. The four features of environmental politics are lists. In association with each of these features is: the relationship of the feature to elements of the model, how the model represents structural change and the effect of structural change on environmental quality.

Table 2-1

The relationship between the four features of environmental politics and the functions represented in Figures 2-2 through 2-6, with examples of structural change

Feature of Environmental Politics	Function	Example of Change Causing Shift in Function	Effect of Shift on Air Quality
Citizen Activism	E	Environmentalism increases in importance	Improve
	P	Perceived threat of environmentalist increases	Worsen
A Seemingly Unresponsive Bureaucracy	R	EPA mandates stricter standards	Improve
	C1	Activists are not allowed standing to bring litigation	Worsen
Normative Conflict	Relationship among $M(P)$, $M(R)$ and $M(E1)$	A new regulator takes a more environmentalist stance	Improve
		A new regulator takes a more pro-business stance	Worsen
Exfoliation	R	Causes are specified, allowing identification of effective action	Improve
		Scientific uncertainty allows business to doubt monger	Worsen

THE LIMITS OF PARTIAL EQUILIBRIUM

There is a glaring omission from the discussion so far. The account that introduced this chapter featured the effect of business only offstage. In the discussion of the four features of environmental politics, business activity only stands in the background. And in the model developed in the preceding section, business activity appears only as one among contending interests.

This is consistent with mainstream, utilitarian economic theory. Business is in an important sense neutral—its driving force to make money is so simple as to be transparent. Its incentives are equally simple: businesses can be persuaded to take actions that improve environmental quality if taking the action minimizes their costs or increases their revenue.

From a functionalist perspective, the presence of business pervades the problem of environmental degradation. The fundamental contradiction of capitalism is that production that becomes increasingly social in nature becomes at the same time increasingly monopolized by a very few. The decisions over what to produce and how to produce it are not made by those who are affected as direct producers, communities and consumers, but by a small business elite. State institutions may intervene in these production decisions, but intervention is almost exclusively in reaction to a business decision. State intervention is rarely preemptive.

The limitations of the utilitarian model is demonstrated by the mainstream economic concept of externality, critiqued in Chapter 1. In mainstream economic theory, environmental degradation is external to the production process: pollution is an unintended result of production and consumption decisions.[47] The concept is overly egalitarian in treating both business and consumer decisions alike. However, consumer choice is largely determined by business choice: consumers get to choose what business decide to put on the market shelf. Environmental degradation is indeed external to the primary motive of production, which is not the creation of goods but the creation of profit. However, environmental degradation is not external to the production process itself: it is intentionally not included as a goal of production.[48]

The four features of environmental politics are a direct result of the hegemonic position of business institutions and the capitalist class. Citizen activism is persistently required because the ownership of the means of production gives owners the presumptive power and preemptive right to appropriate common resources such as the air. To enjoy environmental goods are not sold as commodities, citizens are forced to wrest them from the primary property rights of capitalists.[49]

The existence of environmental agencies is functionally a part of the hegemony of the capitalist class. The disproportionate influence that the capitalist class and business elites have in the formation of agencies, in the access to legislators and administrators, in their ability to organize around a cause and in their ability to marshall resources in support of that cause is only the beginning. These represent the first and second dimensions of hegemonic power.[50]

In the third dimension of power, professional ideologies circumscribe acceptable actions within the confines of alternatives that assume a growth oriented, capitalist economy. The third dimension manifests itself in the generally accepted view that environmental quality must be traded off for jobs, economic health and material well-being.[51]

The normative conflicts pervasive in environmental politics are quite functional. Few industrial polluters will be found who are alarmed at, for example, the respiratory effects of airborne toxic substances. Although Shakespeare's Richard III had the courage to be intentionally evil, polluters do not recognize their acts as indictable. Environmental activists are excessively alarmed because they consider themselves victims, are concerned with the effect and indignant about their involuntary sacrifice. Legislators and bureaucrats, removed from the emotions engendered by the material conditions that motivate activists and elevated by superior technical expertise, must play the role of arbiter between these two competing interests.

The exfoliation of knowledge about environmental problems comes about because at each step in implementing policy, the regulatory institutions discover something new out about the problem. But the problem is one created because business has the power and right to act in a way that is injurious to common resources, and because knowledge of that effect is irrelevant to their decisionmaking. The knowledge of environmental degradation exfoliates because action to improve environmental quality occurs only after the degradation occurs with neither knowledge nor acknowledgement of the consequences.[52]

The model developed in the last section is affected in four ways by the pervasive, hegemonic power of the capitalist class. The first of these is rather obvious. The social forces seeking to prevent regulators from doing "too much" have both a greater willingness and ability to impose costs than do the forces who impose costs on regulators for doing "too little." In Figure 2-4, the "polluter" willingness to impose costs on regulators for doing "too much" function **P** dominates the "environmentalist" willingness to impose costs of regulators for doing "too little" function **E**. As a consequence, the net marginal cost function **C'** that regulators face is predominantly positive and steeply so. The function **C1'** in Figure 2-5 not only dominates, but comes close to resembling the "polluter" function **P'**. The level of management activity, therefore, is in the neighborhood of *M(1)* or even *M(P)*. This tends to reduce the range of management activities regulators will engage in by insuring the sensitivity of regulators to actions which "go overboard."

The irony of this, of course, is that business derives the resources to engage in lobbying, independent research, public relations and other political activities by selling commodities to consumers. Some consumers are the environmentalists who must forego other things to pose a counterforce to business. And virtually all consumers must bear the costs of environmental degradation. The consumer pays twice—for the degradation and for the commodity whose revenue funds the business politics which in turn resist efforts to abate the degradation. The consumer as environmental activist pays three times—for the degradation, for their own efforts to abate the degradation and for the resistance to such efforts through the purchase of commodities.

Second, the regulator's willingness to act is heavily circumscribed by professional ideology. Only management activities which do not challenge the preemptive right of business are acceptable. This is not a case of slavish devotion to the needs of the capitalist class. Nor is it simply a matter of values inculcated through professional training and etiquette. This latter is reinforced by real politics—if Jeb Stuart had "gone overboard", he would have been fired. Such a threat is neither speculative nor apocryphal. In the next chapter we will see how Jeb Stuart's predecessor at the Riverside Air Pollution Control District lost his job. Thus the range of management activities over which the function **R** spans is quite narrow and the response function **R'** is very inelastic—large values in the willingness of the regulator to act cover small changes in management activity. This means that great effort is required to move the regulator away from her preferred course of action *M(R)*, but the resulting increment in management activity is small.

Third, polluters are relatively insensitive to environmental management activities. The response function **q** represented in Figure 2-7 is quite flat, so that there is little difference in the rate of change in environmental quality as a result of alternative levels of management activity. The insensitivity is not simply because environmental regulators have not had the benefit of the effluent fees that mainstream economists have so fervently recommended. Imposition of the real costs of pollution on the activities which create it would be a substantial improvement. However, in functionalist theory the problem goes beyond offering business incentives to prevent environmental degradation. As a matter of principle, business will resist public intervention that does not further its dollars and cents interests. And business will resist public intervention that restricts its rights and powers in controlling the means of production. Business will look for ways to avoid penalization rather than ways to improve environmental quality. They will make their business plans and then determine what action to take in response to environmental regulation.

Fourth, the driving force behind environmental reform, citizen activism, is circumscribed by hegemonic power. There are two dimensions to this limitation: practical and normative. From a practical point of view, activists want to be effective. As a consequence, they will direct their limited energies toward limited yet achievable goals rather than more radical but seemingly hopeless causes. Even if they do recognize institutional limitations and prefer radical change, they may settle for minor improvements in order to be effective at all. Institutional alternatives will be further limited by the generally local focus of environmental activism. For example, in the early days of air pollution control in Los Angeles it was legally possible for regulators to control automobile emissions. Because of the extreme difficulty of achieving such control, activist energies were directed toward more accessible stationary source control.

Normatively, activists are limited by their own class background. For the most part, environmental activists are white, upper middle class (in background if not in current social status) and well educated. They will tend to view environmental quality as another among the goods which ought to be available from the social system that provides them with their high standard of living—and which is in fact dominated by corporate capitalism. That is, the prime movers in environmental activism will be normatively inclined to reform rather than radical change.[53]

The result of hegemonic power in these four forms is that apparently dramatic changes in the incentive structure of environmental regulation will not result in correspondingly dramatic changes in environmental quality. Using Figure 2-5, the rate of change of environmental quality is narrowly defined—the difference between $q1$ and $q2$ in Figure 2-7 is very small. First, the ability of polluters to influence environmental policy and administration dominate—the limit of "too much" is reached quickly and meets with massive resistance. Second, administrators are prepared through professional ideologies to further limit the range of acceptable management activities. Third, polluters have the preemptive right to pollute because their decisions are made without regard to environmental consequences.

SUMMARY AND CONCLUSION

There are four features of environmental politics relevant to the study of air pollution control in Southern California. The first feature is the prominent role played by environmental activism. When environmental issues get on the political agenda, it is the result of citizen activism. Moreover, throughout its history the regulatory effort has been pushed by such activism. Environmental activists generally are people who are directly affected by a specific environmental degradation and who regard the perpetrators of the degradation as betrayers of a public trust.

The second feature is the seeming unresponsiveness of public institutions to environmental degradation. Given the technical complexity of environmental problems, the professionals who administer the implementation of environmental policy regard the solutions as something best left to the experts. They are moreover trained to balance the interests of polluters along with the interests of the polluted. The role professionals take on for themselves is not that of environmental advocate but of technical problem-solver and facilitator of interest group conflict.

The third feature is the normative conflict inherent in environmental politics. How someone views the problem of environmental degradation is functionally related to her functional role. Environmental activists, as victims, regard environmental degradation with the greatest alarm. Polluters, as perpetrators, regard the economic effect of activist successes as of far greater concern than the degradation itself. When placed in a position that requires them to balance these conflicting interests while maintaining their professional objectivity, regulators must not be as sanguine as those they regulate, but nevertheless must regard environmentalist alarm as excessive and even irresponsible.

The fourth feature of environmental regulation is the exfoliation of knowledge of the environmental degradation. Above and beyond normative issues, the very nature of the problem depends on the interaction of science and the institutions of public choice. Knowledge of what must be done to abate environmental degradation only emerges from the attempt to abate itself.

Although the utilitarian model developed in this chapter is helpful in explaining these phenomena, such a model overlooks their functional explanation. The features described are a direct consequence or even a part of the hegemonic power of the capitalist class. The model predicts far too much responsiveness in the political economy to structural changes in institutions affecting environmental quality.

The utilitarian model bases its explanatory power on the idea that legislated mandates to agencies are subject to considerable discretion on the part of the administrators who implement the legislation. This discretionary power operates as a set of trade-offs that are within the control of the regulator: trade-offs of air quality against other goods; trade-offs that are based on the regulator's own career objectives.

The critique of the utilitarian model is that the hegemony of capitalist institutions, such as those of environmental control, are superstructural—where they do not exist to actively support the accumulation of capital, they exist to prevent the abatement of accumulation. Capitalist institutions tend toward stability and the preemptive power and right of capitalist class interests over production decisions.

NOTES

1. Los Angeles *Times* [1981].

2. Mr. Stuart retired in June 1986, becoming a consultant to many of the companies he formerly was responsible for regulating.

3. California State Assembly, Committee On Energy And Natural Resource. n.d.

4. There is a division of labor in air pollution control in California: local districts are responsible for the control of stationary sources of air pollution; CARB, the state agency, is responsible for the regulation of mobile sources of air pollution (primarily automobiles). However, the state agency also has several oversight responsibilities for the regulation of stationary sources—in particular, CARB is responsible for the State Implementation Plan, required by the Federal Clean Air Act. The state plan must specify to the Environmental Protection Agency how the air pollution from all sources will be regulated so that Federal air quality standards are met.

5. Riverside (California) *Press-Enterprise* [1981].

6. Ibid.

7. California Air Resources Board. September 1981.

8. And now congressperson.

9. Mr. Levine was also a prime mover behind the hearings at which the District's Board Chair and Executive Officer felt themselves so unfairly criticized.

10.   California State Assembly, Committee On Energy And Natural Resources. [n.d.: 7-8]

11.   Now District Attorney for Los Angeles County.

12.   Ibid. page 9.

13.   Los Angeles *Times* [1981].

14.   Ibid.

15.   Riverside *Press-Enterprise* [1981].

16.   Who would later sit on the Board of Directors as an alternate to Riverside County Supervisor Norton Younglove.

17.   Orttung [1981].   Orttung would later sit on the Board of Directors as an alternate to Riverside County Supervisor Norton Younglove.

18.   Meade [1981].

19.   These three counties considered themselves victims of the aerial effluents produced in Los Angeles County and transported by wind currents into their jurisdiction. This is especially true of San Bernardino and Riverside Counties. With the rapid grow of Orange County in the 1970s, Riverside considered itself a double victim by being upwind of both Los Angeles and Orange County.

20.   One member would be appointed by the Speaker of the State Assembly, the other by the State Senate Rules Committee—which effectively means appointment by the President Pro Tem of the Senate.

21.   Hays [1980].

22.   Caldwell, Hayes and MacWhirter [1976].

23.   Berry [1977].

24.   Bellah, et al [1985].

25.   Hays [1987].

26.   Caulfield [1989].

27.   Dryzek and Lester [1989].

28.   Caldwell, Hayes and MacWhirter [1976 : xvii].

29.   Caldwell, Hayes and MacWhirter [1976 : xiii-xiv].

30.   Caldwell, Hayes and MacWhirter [1976 : xxix-xxx].

31.   At least as that job is conceived by analysts sympathetic to the concerns of citizen activists.

32.   See Mueller [1989] and [1979].

33.   This arrangement was by no means unprecedented. Prior to the creation of the South Coast Air Quality Management District, the Boards of Supervisors of each county sat as the governing board of the county's Air Pollution Control District. The functional relationship to the agency bureaucracy was essentially the same as with SCAQMD.

34.   Builder and Graubard [1982]. Although completed in January, the report was not accepted by the SCAQMD until much later. The final version was not published until September, 1982. However, nothing of substance differs between the January and September versions. The delay was a result of SCAQMD's reluctance to pay the $75,000 for a study that is regarded as having dubious value.

35.   Builder and Graubard [1982 : 13].

36. Many 'environmental' issues, especially those predating the 1960's, were not organized as environmental issues but as health issues, community control issues, quality of one's neighborhood issues, etc. Samuel Hays notes that

> The office in the US Public Health Service which first dealt with air pollution was called the office of "Community Programs." Hays [1980:722].

37. On Southern California in particular, see Mix [1968]. At the time he wrote the article, Mix was Assistant County Counsel for the County of Los Angeles. On this 'efficiency' approach generally see Grinder [1980] and Schultz and McShane [1980]. The phrase 'constructive engagement' was used by President Ronald Reagan to describe his administration's policy toward the racist institution of apartheid in the Republic of South Africa. The basic concept was to keep a dialogue open so that moral suasion could prevail over palpably anti-social institutions.

38. Sinclair [1980].

39. Krier and Ursin [1977:289].

40. And to a very large extent after 1970 as well.

41. Krier and Ursin [1977:289].

42. Walter Rosenbaum aptly entitles a chapter "Pick a Number: Science, Politics and Environment." Rosenbaum [1985].

43. See the introduction in Baden and Stroup [1981] and Chapter 6 in Downing [1984].

Hays [1981].

45. The function **P** may be thought of as that portion of the producer's surplus allocated to influence environmental politics. Likewise with the function **E1** which represents the portion of the consumer's surplus devoted to environmental politics.

46. The equilibrium at *M(2)* is stable even though it in a region where the regulator's marginal willingness to act is negative. As the level of management increases beyond the regulator's optimal level *M(R)*, the decrease in desirability for each increment in activity becomes greater—undesirable at an increasing rate. Correspondingly, as the level of management increases, environmentalists are less willing to impose costs for an additional increment in management activity. At levels less than *M(2)*, the decrease in the environmentalists' willingness to impose costs for increments in management activity is greater than the decreased desirability for the regulator. The regulator will have an incentive to increase his or her activity until the decreased willingness of environmentalist to impose costs just equals the decrease in desirability of an increment in management activity. A symmetric argument holds for management levels greater than *M(2)*.

47. Baumol and Oates [1975:16-18].

48. Kapp [1974] and [1971].

49. Bromley [1978].

50. Schultz and McShane [1980]; Quirk [1981]; Dear and Scott [1981].

51. Alpert and Markusen [1979]; Hays [1981]; Galambos [1983]; Sinclair [1980].

52. Rosenbaum [1985].

53. Hays [1987].

REFERENCES

Alpert, Irvine and Markusen, Ann. 1979. The professional production of policy, ideology , and plans: Brookings and Resources for the Future. *Insurgent sociologist.* 9 (1979), 94-106.

Baden, John and Stroup, Richard L. 1981. *Bureaucracy vs. environment: the environmental costs of bureaucratic governance.* Ann Arbor: University of Michigan.

Bardach, Eugene and Kagan, Robert A eds. 1982. *Social regulation: strategies for reform.* San Francisco: Institute for Contemporary Studies.

Baumol, William J. and Oates, Wallace E. 1975. *The theory of environmental policy: externalities, public outlays and the quality of life.* Englewood Cliffs, NJ: Prentice-Hall.

Bellah, Robert N., et al. 1985. *Habits of the heart: individualism and commitment in American life.* New York: Harper and Row.

Berman, David R. 1982. Consumerism and the regulatory system: paradigms of reform. *Policy Studies Review.* 1:3 (1982), 454-462.

Berry, William D. 1982. Theories of regulatory impact. *Policy Studies Review.* 1:3 (1982), 436-441.

Berry, Jeffrey M. 1982. Citizen groups and alternative approaches to regulatory reform. *Policy Studies Review.* 1:3 (1982), 503-509.

Berry, Jeffrey M. 1977. *Lobbying for the people: the political behavior of public interest groups.* Princeton:Princeton University.

Breton, Albert and Wintrobe, Ronald. 1982. *The logic of bureaucratic conduct.* Cambridge:Cambridge University.

Bromley, Daniel W. 1978. Property rules, liability rules, and environmental economics. *Journal of economic issues.* 7:1 (March, 1978), 43-60.

Builder, Carl H. and Graubard, Morlie H. 1982. A conceptual approach to strategies for the control of air pollution in the South Coast Air Basin. Santa Monica: Rand.

Caldwell, Lynton K., Hayes, Lynton R. and MacWhirter, Isabel M. 1976. *Citizens and the environment: case studies in popular action.* Bloomington: University of Indiana.

California Air Resources Board. 1981. Adequacy, effectiveness, and potential for improvement in air pollution enforcement.

California State Assembly, Committee On Energy And Natural Resources. n.d.. Air quality in the South Coast Air Basin: staff background paper. n.d.

Caulfield, Henry P. 1989. The conservation and environmental movements: an historical analysis. Lester, James P., ed. 1989. *Environmental politics and policy: theories and evidence.* Durham: Duke. 13-56.

Cockburn, Alexander and Ridgeway, James eds. 1979. *Political ecology: and activist's reader on energy, land, food, technology, heal.* New York: New York Times Books.

Commoner, Barry. 1990. *Making peace with the planet.* New York: Pantheon.

Commoner, Barry. 1971. *The closing circle: nature, man and technology.* New York: Bantam.

Davies, J. Clarence and Davies, Barbara S. 1975. *The politics of pollution.* Indianapolis, IN: Pegasus.

Dear, Michael and Scott, Allen J. eds. 1981. *Urbanization and urban planning in capitalist society.* New York: Methuen.

Downing, Paul. 1984. *Environmental economics and policy.* Boston: Little, Brown and Company.

Dryzek, John S. and Lester, James P. 1989. Alternative views of the environmental problem. Lester, James P., ed. 1989. *Environmental politics and policy: theories and evidence.* Durham: Duke. 314-330.

Dubnick, Mel and Gitelson, Alan R. 1982. Regulatory policy analysis: working in a quagmire. *Policy Studies Review.* 1:3 (1982), 423-435.

Edel, Matthew. 1973. *Economies and the environment.* Englewood Cliffs, NJ: Prentice-Hall.

Edsall, Thomas Byrne. 1984. *The new politics of inequality.* New York: W.W. Norton and Company.

Fisher, Anthony C. 1981. *Resource and environmental economics.* Cambridge: Cambridge University.

Friedlaender, Ann ed. 1978. *Approaches to controlling air pollution.* Cambridge, MA: MIT.

Galambos, Louis. 1983. Technology, political economy and professionalism: central themes of the organizational synthesis. *Business history review.* 57:4 (Winter, 1983), 471-493.

Gorz, Andre. 1980. *Ecology as politics.* Boston: South End.

Grinder, Dale R. 1980. The battle for clean air: the smoke problem in post-Civil War America. Melosi, Martin V, ed. *Pollution and reform in American cities, 1870-1930.* Austin: University of Texas. 83-104.

Grinder, Dale R. 1978. From insurgency to efficiency: the smoke abatement campaign in Pittsburgh before World War I. *The western Pennsylvania historical magazine.* 61:3 (July, 1978), 187-202.

Hahn, Robert W. and McRae, Gregory J. 1982. Application of market mechanisms to pollution. *Policy Studies Review.* 1:3 (1982), 470-476.

Hays, Samuel P. 1987. *Beauty, health, and permanence: environmental politics in the United States, 1955-1985.* Cambridge: Cambridge.

Hays, Samuel P. 1981. Political choice in regulatory administration. McCraw, Thomas K.,ed. *Regulation in perspective: historical essays.* Boston: Harvard University Press. 124-154.

Hays, Samuel P. 1980. The structure of environmental politics since World War II. *Journal of social history.* 14:1 (1980), 719-738.

Hays, Samuel P. 1979. Clean air: from the 1970 Act to the 1977 Amendments. *Duquesne Law Review.* 17 (1979), 33-66.

Hays, Samuel P. 1959. *Conservation and the gospel of efficiency: the Progressive conservation movement.* New York: Atheneum.

Hilton, George. 1972. The basic behavior of regulatory commissions. *American economic review.* 62:2 (May, 1972), 47-54.

Juergensmeyer, Julian C. and Wadley, James B.. 1974. The common lands concept: a "commons" solution to a common environmental problem. *Natural resources journal.* 14 (July, 1974), 361-381.

Kapp, K. William. 1974. *Environmental policies and development planning in contemporary China and other essays.* The Hague: Monton.

Kapp, K. William. 1971. *The social costs of private enterprise.* New York: Schocken.

Katzmann, Robert. 1980. *Regulatory bureaucracy.* Cambridge, MA: MIT.

Kolko, Gabriel. 1963. *The triumph of conservatism.* New York: Harper and Row.

Krier, James E. and Ursin, Edmund. 1977. *Pollution and policy: a case essay on California and Federal experience with motor vehicle pollution control, 1940-1975.* Berkeley: University of California.

Larson, Magali Sarfatti. 1977. *The rise of professionalism: a sociological analysis.* Berkeley: University of California.

Lester, James P., ed. 1989. *Environmental politics and policy: theories and evidence.* Durham: Duke.

Los Angeles *Times.* 1981. Air quality district accused of laxity. Part II (September 24, 1981), 1.

Marcus, Alfred A., Sommers, Paul and Morris, Frederic A. 1982. Alternative arrangements for cost effective pollution abatement. *Policy studies review.* 1:3 (1982), 477-483.

McCraw, Thomas K. 1974. Regulation in America: a review article. *Business history review.* 49:2 (Summer, 1974), 159-183.

McCraw, Thomas K. ed. 1981. *Regulation in perspective: historical essays.* Boston: Harvard University Press.

Meade, Gladys. 1981. Statement to the California State Assembly Committee on Energy and Natural Resources.

Melosi, Martin V. ed. 1980. *Pollution and reform in American cities, 1870-1930.* Austin: University of Texas.

Mitnick, Barry M. 1982. Regulation and the theory of agency. *Policy studies review.* 1:3 (1982), 442-453.

Mix, David D. 1968. The misdemeanor approach to pollution control. *Arizona law review.* 10 (1968), 90-96.

O'Riordan, T. 1976. *Environmentalism.* London: Pion.

Orttung, Judy. 1981. Statement to the California State Assembly Committee on Energy and Natural Resources.

Pearce, D.W. 1976. *Environmental economics.* London: Longman.

Peltzman, Sam. 1976. Toward a more general theory of regulation. *The journal of law and economics.* 19:2 (August, 1976), 211-248.

Petulla, Joseph M. 1977. *American environmental history: the exploitation and conservation of natural resources.* San Francisco: Boyd and Fraser.

Quirk, Paul J. 1981. *Industry influence in Federal regulatory agencies.* Princeton: Princeton University.

Riverside Press-Enterprise. 1981. Critics level charges at air quality district final hearing day. Section B (September 24, 1981), 1.

Rosenbaum, Walter. 1985. *Environmental politics and policy.* Washington, D.C.: Congressional Quarterly.

Rowland, C.K. and Marz, Roger. 1982. Gresham's Law: the regulatory analogy. *Policy studies review.* 1:3 (1982), 572-580.

Sabatier, Paul. 1975. Social movements and regulatory agencies: toward a more adequate--and less pessimistic--theory of "clientele capture". *Policy studies.* 6 (1975), 301-342.

Sandbach, Francis. 1982. *Principles of pollution control.* London: Longman.

Sandbach, Francis. 1980. *Environment, ideology and policy.* Montclair, NJ: Allanheld, Osmun and Company.

Schnaiberg, Allan. 1980. *The environment: from surplus to scarcity.* Oxford: Oxford University.

Schultz, Stanley K. and McShane, Clay. 1980. Pollution and political reform in urban America: the role of the municipal engineer. Melosi, Martin V, ed. *Pollution and reform in American cities, 1870-1930.* Austin: University of Texas, 1980. 155-172.

Sinclair, Bruce. 1980. *A centennial history of the American Society of Mechanical Engineers, 1880-1980.* Toronto: University of Toronto.

Stretton, Hugh. 1976. *Capitalism, socialism and the environment.* Cambridge: Cambridge University.

Tabb, William K. and Sawers, Larry eds. 1984. *Marxism and the metropolis: new perspective in urban political economy.* Oxford: Oxford University.

Veljanovski, C.G. 1982. The market for regulatory enforcement. *The Economic journal, supplement.* (1982), 123-129.

Walton, Gary M ed. 1979. *Regulatory change in an atmosphere of crisis: current implications of the Roosevelt years.* New York: Academic.

Weisberg, Barry. 1971. *Beyond repair: the ecology of capitalism.* Boston: Beacon.

Wilson, James Q. ed. 1980. *The politics of regulation.* New York: Basic Books.

Yandle, Bruce. 1989. *The political limits of environmental regulation: tracking the unicorn.* New York: Quorum.

CHAPTER 3

Smog In The Port Of Iowa [1]

Discovering the nature of air pollution has been an important part of the history of smog in Southern California.[2] The single most important discovery by scientists was that important air pollutants are not direct effluents of source activity but instead are the product of chemical reactions in the air itself. The physiographic and meteorological characteristics of the South Coast Air Basin contribute to these processes. Meteorological conditions frequently create an inversion layer.[3] This inversion layer acts as a lid on the physiographic bowl of the South Coast Air Basin, trapping effluents that would otherwise escape into the upper atmosphere. Thus immobilized, the solar radiation that otherwise blesses Southern California energizes chemical reactions among effluents, transforming them into photochemical products.

Hence smog is frequently referred to as photochemical smog. The first discoveries of these photochemical processes occurred in the early 1950s. When these discoveries were made and generally accepted, the regulatory focus did not so much shift as expand: regulators had to be concerned with controlling what happened in the air as well as what got put into it.

The first photochemical reaction discovered was that of reactive hydrocarbons[4] with nitrogen oxides in the presence of sunlight—a reaction that produces ozone and other photochemical oxidants. This discovery of photochemical reactions, more than any other, produced a major change in the regulatory effort. Pollution sources would now be scrutinized for both the pollutants they directly produced and the precursors to pollutants created in the air. And the air itself ceased to be a simple receptacle for pollutants, but a caldron of pollution chemistry. As a consequence of these discoveries, means had to be developed to monitor and control the new effluents.

The primary focus of air pollution has always been the combustion of fossil fuels.[5] Until the photochemistry of Southern California's smog was discovered, attention was placed on the release of sulfur and other elements contained in the fuel along with the creation of soot.[6] These pollutants implicated stationary sources[7]—literally combustion processes that do not move. The reason for this dominance was that stationary sources tended to use fossil fuels with a much higher sulfur content than the gasolines and diesels used by automobiles.

The discovery that reactive hydrocarbons and nitrogen oxides

Table 3-I

Effluents over the driving cycle

Phase Of Driving Cycle	Exhaust Flow Volume	Effluent Concentration	
		Reactive Hydrocarbons	Nitrogen Oxides
Idle	Very Low	High	Very Low
Cruise			
Low Speed	Low	Low	Low
High Speed	High	Very Low	Moderate
Accelerate			
Moderate	High	Low	High
Heavy	Very High	Moderate	Moderate
Decelerate	Very Low	Very High	Very Low

Adapted from Table 9-1 in Lynn [1976:243].

played the major role in producing smog dramatically shifted attention to Los Angeles' teeming population of automobiles. The reason for this is summarized in Table 3-I.

The table shows what happens over the driving cycle—a cycle that is repeated at least once each time a motor vehicle is used.   As the table indicates, from the standpoint of hydrocarbon and nitrogen oxide production, the optimal place in the driving cycle is in low speed cruise.[8] By the very nature of motor vehicle use, this stage constitutes only a fraction of the time spent while a vehicle is in use.[9] This feature of the motor vehicle driving cycle makes sense of the support initially given to the development of the freeway system as a panacea to smog: street driving entails numerous repetitions of the driving cycle; ideally, freeway driving entails both fewer repetitions of the cycle with an increase in the amount of time spent in the cruise phase of the cycle.

There are other ironies associated with the basic photochemistry of Southern California's smog. One irony is that the production of nitrogen oxides and hydrocarbons is linked in a perverse way: generally, low hydrocarbon output implies high nitrogen oxide production. The perversity is compounded when the relationship between performance and effluents is examined: fuel efficient combustion results in peak nitrogen oxide production, optimal power output results in peak hydrocarbon output. Thus through the incentive to maximize fuel economy or power, effluents are perversely maximized.

Another irony, which leads back to the nature of the regulatory environment, occurs when oxidants other than ozone are produced in the atmosphere of Southern California—resulting in the formation of a West Coast equivalent of acid rain. On the East Coast, acid rain result from the discharge of oxides of sulfur from the burning of high sulfur fuels, especially coal. The sulfur oxides are transformed in the air into sulfuric acid. In contrast, Southern California was able to reduce the use of high sulfur fuels economically. As a consequence, the high volume of sulfur oxides virtually disappeared soon after the regulation of air quality began.

However, research by scientists at the California Institute of Technology discovered an equally serious problem: the atmospheric formation of nitric acid from nitrogen oxides.[10] As it turns out, technically, nitrogen oxides are not uniquely associated with mobile sources in the way that hydrocarbons are; moreover, as compared to both sulfur dioxide and hydrocarbons, nitrogen oxides have been more difficult to abate from a purely technical standpoint.

A final demonstration of the salience of scientific discovery in regulating Southern California's smog was the recent organization of a

$10 million research project involving 200 scientists.[11] The objective of the study was to use the South Coast Air Basin as a living laboratory on the atmospheric chemistry and atmospheric transport of air pollution.[12]

THE BAY OF SMOKES [13]

Air pollution emerged as an issue in Los Angeles during World War II.[14] The specific incident that is traditionally cited to mark this emergence occurred during July, 1943. A gale of complaints descended on Los Angeles City and County government offices when an "acrid ozone" had appeared in the downtown area. Inspectors from both the City and County Health Departments were sent out to investigate the complaints. Their investigation revealed,

> a brew of "ammonia, formaldehyde, acrolein, acetic acid, sulfuric acid, sulfur dioxide, hydrogen sulfide, mercaptans, hydrochloric acid, hydrofluoric acid, chlorine, nitric acid, phosgene, and certain organic dusts known to be irritants," for which scores of sources, ranging from fish canneries to oil refineries, could be blamed.[15]

Attention finally fell on a plant in downtown Los Angeles that produced butadiene as part of the War Industry Board's Rubber Reserve Corporation.[16]

In concluding his investigation of the incident, Dr. George Uhl, Los Angeles City Health Officer, reported to the City Council that the fundamental problem was not the butadiene plant itself, but the phenomena of which the plant was a part: the combination of industrial growth and atmospheric conditions was at the bottom of these "gas attacks." The City Engineer's office reported to the Council that the butadiene plant was the sole culprit. The City Council remanded Dr. Uhl's report to a committee, where it died of neglect.[17]

Eventually the Rubber Reserve was forced to close the butadiene plant after a series of broken promises and further "gas attacks." However, as a consequence of the incident and the portents it raised, the Los Angeles County Board of Supervisors created a Smoke And Fumes Commission in October, 1943.[18] In a little over a year the Commission produced a report that consisted of a model ordinance and a set of recommendations for hiring the staff necessary to implement the ordinance. However, the intervening course of events did not lead the Commissioners to optimism.

The chairman of the Commission, Al Waxman, acknowledged "how deeply involved this problem is in politics."[19]   In his letter of transmission, Dr. William Clapp exuded pessimism. He observed that the lack of data would impede swift action or the allocation of sufficient funding to investigate the problem adequately. He then went on to say that, "even if this information were at hand, your Commission is beginning to doubt whether any effective ordinance for control of fumes would ever be enacted."[20]

The referent for these complaints was another Smoke and Fumes Commission, which had been created by the Los Angeles County Chamber of Commerce shortly after the creation of the County Commission. The Board of Supervisors had the business-conscious Chamber Commission work with their own Commission on the model ordinance. A deeper problem emerged in that the County Commission had become quite ambitious in outlining the scientific and institutional needs required to deal with the smog problem.

Upon receipt of the County Commission's final report, Supervisors William Smith and Roger Jessup moved to have Mr. Waxman fired from the County Smoke and Fumes Commission. They claimed that the rest of the Commission was dissatisfied with Waxman's participation and chairmanship. This claim was news not only to Mr. Waxman, but to the other members of the Commission as well. In late January, 1945, after failing to remove Mr. Waxman, Supervisor Jessup led a unanimous County Board of Supervisors in abolishing the Commission itself. Mr. Waxman asserted that "certain members of the Board of Supervisors have been more concerned over the desires of the Los Angeles Chamber of Commerce than they have over the desires of the requirements of the man-in-street [sic]."   Dr. Vivian concurred, observing that "it seems that certain interests do not want any control on smoke and fumes."[21]

Marvin Brienes claims that "the best organized effort, in fact, was launched by the Los Angeles Chamber of Commerce."[22]   The Chamber's Smoke and Fumes Commission was created in October, 1944 as an expansion of the Industrial Zoning Committee to include "realtors, railroad officials, representatives from the fuel oil industry, public utilities, eleven city and county agencies and the District Attorney."[23] In addition to criticizing and subsequently causing delays in the County Commission's final report and model ordinance, the Chamber's Commission began "a campaign for the voluntary abatement of smoke and fumes by commercial and industrial establishments."[24]

Once an ordinance was actually passed by the County in February, 1945, the Chamber was further effective in neutralizing a good part of its potential effect because of a jurisdictional feature of county ordinances. The California State Code of Civil Procedures allowed county ordinances to apply only to unincorporated areas of the county. Efforts were being made to exempt the air pollution ordinance so it would apply to incorporated areas as well—the areas with the heaviest industrial development.

> California nuisance law provided at this time that if a factory were located in an area where, under a local zoning ordinance, manufacturing uses were permitted, then the factory's pollution could not be enjoined as a nuisance unless proved to be the result of unnecessary operations. This provision applied on its face to many pollution sources the district attorney hoped to abate.... During the 1945 session of the legislature, he sought an amendment that would have excepted from the statute "an action to abate a public nuisance brought in the name of the people of the state of California." The measure passed the Assembly, then died in the Senate Committee, thanks largely to the opposition of the Los Angeles Chamber of Commerce and the Merchants and Manufacturers Association.[25]

Both the City and County hired Air Pollution Control Officers and supporting staffs whose first actions were to investigate how to effectively control the problem.

Even at this early date in the smog control program individuals both inside and outside the government began to realize the problem was more complex than just black smoke.[26]

However, the explicit orientation of the enforcement program promoted the education and persuasion of polluters rather than the enforcement of standards through civil suits. This educate-and-persuade approach was an extension of the existing Chamber of Commerce program.

In mid-1947, Los Angeles City industry was reported to have invested more than $3.5 million to help end smog. [The County's] office, with far fewer factories in its purview, reported "sincere co-operation" from industrial plants. City officials, who in 1944 termed co-operation "good," were now saying it was "splendid."[27]

The educate-and-persuade approach was consistent with the attack on air pollution as a smoke problem. Traditional smoke abatement problems and programs in other cities had been defined as engineering problems—the result of inefficiencies. The practitioners and promoters of smoke abatement efforts were perceived as industrial services in disguise.[28]

Los Angeles's industries were willing to cooperate, explained Dr. Uhl, because "black smoke indicated inefficiency," and most persistent violators of the smoke ordinances were presumably those marginal producers who did not command the engineering talent necessary to prevent profits from going up in their smoke.[29]

Despite all of these valiant efforts the jurisdictional problems persisted, leading to the promotion and passage in 1947 of state legislation that allowed for the creation of a county-wide Air Pollution Control District. There were two sources of opposition to the bill that would create the new APCDs. Business opposition came from the railroad and lumber industries, while public opposition came from cities within Los Angeles County. The business opposition was overcome by a threat from Norman Chandler, owner and publisher of the Los

Angeles *Times*, to give the businesses a bad press. The city opposition—led by the City of Los Angeles and based on the view that the APCDs would not adequately regulate businesses—dissipated because the proposed legislation was better than nothing and championing an alternative would take more effort and resources than could be mustered. The Los Angeles County APCD went into operation in June, 1947.[30]

At the time that the Los Angeles APCD was created, the only atmospheric effluent with any research history to speak of was sulphur dioxide. It therefore made considerable sense that the first Air Pollution Control Officer, Louis McCabe, was hired from the Bureau of Mines where the bulk of this research had taken place.[31]

McCabe made it clear that his task was to set up the new agency, get it started, then return to the Bureau of Mines. The approach he followed continued the time-honored tradition of organizing the agency around the twin objectives of enforcement action and research. Although he dropped the interest the Los Angeles City Air Pollution Control Officer, Isador Deutch, had shown in the automobile, he did continue and even expand work with local universities. However, the scale was nowhere close to the plan Mr. Deutch had envisioned.

Once the agency became staffed, and research underway, McCabe turned to enforcement. Despite opposition from the Western Oil And Gas Association, McCabe implemented regulatory standards for a number of pollutants. The Association had argued unsuccessfully that

> the problem is a scientific one, to ascertain what is smog and what are the contributing factors, what is causing the eye-smarting and throat irritation under certain climatic conditions and what affects visibility under certain climatic conditions in addition to the natural fog. We feel it is premature to be setting up standards of tolerance before knowing what is causing the conditions. No precedents are available to guide us.... We have no precedent and that is why I stress that there should be a thorough scientific study before arriving at conclusions.[32]

Just before Mr. McCabe returned to the Bureau of Mines, he informed the Los Angeles City Council that the smog problem would be gone in a short time—between eight and fourteen months. McCabe was replaced by his assistant Gordon Larson.

One of the research projects McCabe initiated went to Arie Haagen-Smit of the California Institute of Technology. Haagen-Smit had been recommended by fellow CalTech faculty member Arnold Beckman, an active member of the Los Angeles County Chamber of Commerce and later founder of Beckman Instruments. By 1951 Haagen-Smit had published his results showing the role of reactive hydrocarbons and nitrogen oxides in the formation of ozone.

At the same time that the APCD enlisted Haagen-Smit, the Western Oil and Gas Association (WOGA) went shopping for its own researchers. WOGA found them at the Stanford Research Institute (SRI). When Haagen-Smit produced his results, SRI attempted and failed to reproduce them. A controversy then ensued which was unofficially settled by 1955, but officially not settled until the final report of the Southern California Air Pollution Foundation in 1958.

The Foundation[33] was the creation of a consortium of business organizations and public officials brought together by Arnold Beckman. Beckman was completing his task as chairman of an investigative committee created by Governor Goodwin Knight in 1953. Knight had been forced to act because of some very forceful lobbying by Fletcher Bowron, Mayor of Los Angeles, over the apparent inadequacy of the APCD's efforts. The purpose of the so-called Beckman Committee was two-fold: investigate the enforcement and administrative practices of the APCD; and settle the controversy surrounding Haagen-Smit's findings.

Gordon Larson, as Air Pollution Control Officer, had been acting on Haagen-Smit's findings since their publications. Larson had also pursued the implementation of a policy to restrict the control of more traditional forms of air pollution through the elimination of incinerators as a form of trash disposal—including the thousands of individual backyard incinerators. Unfortunately, Larson was an almost classic technocrat; generally regarded as highly competent technically, politically he managed to alienate virtually everyone with the unpopular control measures he proposed.

In 1955 Larson was fired and replaced by Smith Griswold, an Assistant to the County Administrative Officer. At this time a number of pieces came together: first, Griswold, although lacking technical background, was politically very savvy; second, the cause of the APCD would be championed on the Board of Supervisors by newly elected

Warren Dorn[34]; third, Haagen-Smit's findings implicating the role of the automobile were being vindicated; fourth, newly-elected Supervisor Kenneth Hahn began what would turn out to be a long-term engagement with the Automobile Manufacturer's Association over what they intended to do about the smog problem; and finally, State and Federal health agencies were becoming involved in the air pollution issue in a limited way.

By the late 1950s Griswold had succeeded in creating a series of regulations affecting stationary sources in the South Coast Air Basin. These included the elimination of all incinerators, through the implementation of a massive solid waste disposal system adopted by the Board of Supervisors; the implementation of the first in a series of fuel control measures that in a decade would eliminate entirely the use of fuels with a high sulfur content; the implementation of a health warning system for potentially harmful smog episodes; and removing responsibility for the control of automobile-generated air pollution from the purview of the local agency.

By 1960 the demarcation in source control was clearly in place: the State had created the Motor Vehicle Pollution Control Board; the three major automobile manufacturer's, under the aegis of the Automobile Manufacturer's Association, were conducting joint research into exhaust control devices; and the APCD successfully claimed that mobile sources accounted for 80% to 90% of the smog in the South Coast Air Basin. The Los Angeles County Air Pollution Control District was held up as a paragon of environmental research and regulation—the successful merging of science and politics.

By 1970 this picture had changed dramatically: the Los Angeles APCD, and especially the administrative apparatus that supports it, was being criticized for its technical backwardness and for being the creature of the industries it supposedly controlled. A series of political events would add to the escalation of the problems facing the APCD. In 1972 Baxter Ward defeated Supervisor Warren Dorn for re-election by criticizing the performance of the APCD[35] and Dorn's stewardship of the District. In 1974 Los Angeles City Councilmember Ed Edelman, running on an environmentalist platform, was elected to the Board of Supervisors. These political changes were aided by the successful challenge to the claim that 90% of smog was attributable to mobile sources—a claim replaced by a more balanced 60% mobile / 40% stationary split. Cities throughout the South Coast Air Basin were lobbying heavily for a greater say in air pollution control. Outlying counties, especially San Bernardino and Riverside Counties, were most vocal in their complaints against Los Angeles—to the extent that the City of Riverside brought suit in 1972 against the Environmental Protection Agency because Los Angeles was not abiding by the newly enacted Clean Air Act Amendments of 1970.[36] In the end the State legislature would supplant the individual county APCDs in the South Coast Air Basin with the South Coast Air Pollution Control District.

The Los Angeles APCD was doing business as it had been in the 1950s—it had virtually the same staff that it had in the 1950s.[37] An investigation by the California Air Resources Board created under Governor Ronald Reagan and conducted by its chairperson Dr. Arie Haagen-Smit, gave the District a generally good review, with the major criticism being that the administrative staff needed to get off their high horse. The investigation had been initiated by a citizen's suit against the Los Angeles APCD for what amounted to malfeasance.[38] The District's supply function for clean air had remained the same while the demand function for clean air had shifted.

Smith Griswold resigned in 1963, offering grave forebodings upon his departure—although the forebodings had more to do with control of mobile sources than stationary ones. Griswold was replaced by Louis Fuller.[39] Fuller resigned in 1971 to be replaced by Robert Chass. With Chass the administration of the Los Angeles APCD had come full circle—back to a technocrat unskilled at public politics.[40] Under Fuller the District saw the emergence of State and Federal agencies into preeminence over the air pollution issue, and under Chass this supersession, even in the area of stationary source control, was completed.

The legislation that created the South Coast Air Quality Management District (SCAQMD) is commonly referred to as the Lewis Act—after the author of the bill, then State Senator from San Bernardino Jerry Lewis. The Lewis Act was the last in a line of proposed legislation (and ballot initiatives) intended to consolidate and reform air pollution control in Southern California. The Lewis Act unified Orange County with those portions of Los Angeles, Riverside and San Bernardino Counties that lie within the South Coast Air Basin. The Lewis Act passed the California State Assembly and Senate in June, 1976 and was signed by Governor Jerry Brown in July.

SCAQMD, the result of this Act, went into operation in February, 1977.[41]

In 1973 a spate of bills affecting air pollution regulation in California were introduced into both houses of the State Legislature. Among them was a bill by Assembly Speaker Robert Moretti. The bill[42] would have reorganized county Air Pollution Control Districts from county-based jurisdictions to physiographically-based jurisdictions, i.e., agencies would regulate airsheds rather than the counties. Organizationally, the measure would have created a State-wide air pollution control program analogous to California's Coastal Commission or Water Resources Control Board: air pollution regulation (primarily the setting of air quality standards) would have been centralized, while the implementation of plans would be the responsibility of regional governing boards. Moretti's proposal would have brought together all of the counties included within the South Coast Air Basin—i.e., Orange County and the appropriate parts of Los Angeles, Riverside, San Bernardino, Santa Barbara and Ventura Counties.

Several attempts and several vetoes by Governor Ronald Reagan later, a bill originally introduced by San Bernardino State Senator Jerry Lewis in 1975 created the South Coast Air Quality Management District in July, 1976.[43] The creation of SCAQMD had been stalled for a year by the creation of the Southern California Air Pollution Control District—a multi-county entity created under existing air pollution control law. The prime motive for the delay on the part of the counties involved varied: Los Angeles County wanted to maintain control, while Riverside, San Bernardino and Orange Counties wanted consolidation without a State imposed structure. Los Angeles APCD Public Affairs Director James Birakos observed that "our experience has been that control is better at the local level where local politicians are more responsive."[44]

This concern with local control was something of a common thread: one of the major features of the Lewis Act was to provide cities within the South Coast Air Basin, and especially the city of Los Angeles, a voice in air pollution policy making.[45] By this time, Robert Chass had been replace by his lieutenant Robert Lunche. Lunche had described the objective of the Lewis Bill as not air pollution control but rather the control of the life-style and future development of Southern California without public consent.[46]

Lunche was replaced as head of the Southern California Air Pollution Control District by Jeb Stuart. Stuart became head of SCAQMD when it was formed. Stuart had been the Air Pollution Control Officer for Riverside County. He had come to the Riverside APCD from the San Bernardino APCD where he had been the enforcement officer for Kaiser Steel.[47] Stuart also came to the Riverside under unpleasant circumstances: his predecessor, Galen Kinley, had been dismissed on the nominal grounds that he was an inadequate administrator; however, the evidence suggests that he was enforcing the regulations with a little too much alacrity.[48] A Grand Jury Report concluded that the complaints lodged by the District employees alleging Mr. Kinley's administrative short-comings had simply provided an opportunity for the Supervisors to act on behalf of aggrieved air pollution sources. Their insight seems easily generalizable:

> The Supervisors have appointed themselves as the APCD Board and are, consequently, in the untenable position of requiring, on the one hand, that the APCD do its work, but, on the other, that it not do it too well.... The investigating Jurors can only conclude that, although it was Mr. Galen Kinley personally who suffered the internal and external pressures which led to his recent resignation, the circumstances surrounding that resignation would have prevailed had someone else been the [Air Pollution Control Officer]—and they will prevail in the future. This conclusion is based on the assumption that any man hired as [Air Pollution control Officer] of the APCD will be committed to pursuing his duties conscientiously.[49]

As in the replacement of Gordon Larson by Smith Griswold, a technocrat had been replaced by an administrative politician. Before coming to the San Bernardino APCD in 1972, Stuart had been a career Air Force officer with no technical background. In 1975, when Mr. Stuart was promoted to Executive Officer of the Southern California APCD he wanted be thought of as a "conciliator" rather than as a "hardliner."[50] In 1980 as Chief Executive of the South Coast Air Quality Management District, Stuart reiterated the same philosophy:

The Clean Air Act doesn't say we should achieve clean air regardless of the cost. We want to inhibit industrial growth as little as possible without relinquishing our goals.[51]

As the vignette included in the last chapter indicates, as of 1982 considerable concern still remained over the effectiveness of the restructuring of air pollution control in the South Coast Air Quality Management District—this despite a bill of health by the Environmental Protection Agency in 1986 that was akin to the one provided by the Los Angeles APCD in 1973 under Arie Haagen-Smit. By 1987 talk of yet another restructuring was taking place.[52] The clean bill had not negated the fact that the EPA has all but given up on SCAQMD attaining the federally mandated air quality standards.

STATE AND FEDERAL INTERVENTION

The intervention of California state and federal regulation has had the effect of shifting policy-making responsibilities from local jurisdictions to state and federal entities: over the course of the post-War era, the APCDs of California have been moved into the role of enforcers of state and federal will. As Jeb Stuart's remarks suggest, the Los Angeles APCD and SCAQMD have frequently been reluctant to restrict themselves to this role.

The leadership that the Los Angeles APCD had exercised emphasized engineering: the modification of industrial processes so that pollutants would be captured at the smokestack or tailpipe. With the ascendancy of state and federal regulation, there was a major shift away from engineering solutions and toward planning solutions.[53] During the 1960s the field of environmental science and planning had developed to the point where the dominant thinking in the profession centered on what one analyst inelegantly called "social engineering."[54] To use the market analogy, so far as many professionals were concerned the APCD's supply function was supported by an outmoded technology.

In 1959 the Los Angeles Board of Supervisors arranged for the introduction of the legislation that created the California Motor Vehicle Pollution Control Board (MVPCB). The Board of Supervisors seemed to hope that the MVPCB would take the problem of regulating the automobile off of its hands: although nominally the APCD found it difficult to negotiate technical solutions to the automobile emissions problem, they were legally empowered to control emissions until the passage in 1967 of the Mulford-Carrell Act that created the California Air Resources Board in 1967.

The MVPCB went into operation in 1960 and lived its life as a transitional institution: until the time of its creation, the State had been a reluctant participant in the air pollution issue, restricting its role to limited research in the State Health Department. The MVPCB continued to be a research agency, but with a broad mandate for establishing statewide air quality standards—particularly with overseeing the development and installation of effective motor vehicle pollution control devices.

As a "control" agency, however, the MVPCB had serious shortcomings. The automobile industry was heavily involved with the creation of the MVPCB and had lobbied strenuously and effectively in preventing effective enforcement powers, such as an inspection program, to be included in the MVPCB's empowering legislation. The legislation went further in isolating the MVPCB from related State Departments. In order to provide itself with needed information, the Board had to call upon the automobile industry and control agencies for technical advice.[55]

By the mid-1960s the MVPCB was obviously not able to do an adequate job. Although the Mulford-Carrell Act that created the California Air Resources Board (CARB) in 1967 had originally been intended to encompass stationary sources as well as mobile sources, local governments (especially Los Angeles County) effectively restricted the ARB's role to implementing and enforcing mobile source emission standards.[56]

At the Federal level there was a developing competition between Senators Gaylord Nelson and Edmund Muskie over who would be the leading anti-pollution legislator. In 1967 Muskie authored the Clean Air Act, which was passed as a piece of legislation intended primarily to support local efforts at smog control. When the environmental issue was at its peak in 1970 the Act was amended under Muskie's leadership. The 1970 amendments firmly placed the federal government in the leading role in setting mobile and stationary source standards and in establishing enforcement procedures.

The immediate impact was that the automobile industry was put on notice to come up with effective exhaust control devices by 1973 or face severe sanctions. In 1969 the major automobile manufacturers had signed a consent decree in a federal anti-trust suit. The suit claimed that while the consortium that was allegedly working to develop the best exhaust control system was in fact using the relationship to put off controls.[57] California turned out to have standards even stricter than the federal standards, and was in fact allowed to retain those more stringent standards—to the chagrin of the auto makers.

The greatest impact on air pollution control was the requirement that the ARB, by 1972, create a State Implementation Plan that would demonstrate how the ARB and the APCDs were going to achieve the federal standards for air pollution by the specified deadline year of 1978. This meant that the ARB, and after it the EPA, had the right to literally take over the operation of APCDs that did not show adequate progress in meeting the federal standards.

The 1970 amendments provided air pollution control agencies the power to use transportation controls, land use planning, and control over the location and construction of indirect sources that induced polluting activities (such as shopping centers that would increase auto traffic). Not only were air pollution agencies enjoined to achieve the federal standards, but they were also enjoined to prevent the deterioration of air quality where the standards were met or exceeded.[58] It was these provisions that allowed the City of Riverside to sue the EPA in 1972. The suit forced the EPA to come up with a transportation plan for the South Coast Air Basin that met federal standards. The resulting plan indicated that Southern California driving would have to be reduced by 70% by 1978.[59]

This situation was only an exaggerated version of the situation throughout the rest of the United States: many of the provisions of the Clean Air Act Amendments were somewhere between difficult and impossible to achieve. A further set of amendments were enacted in 1977.[60] These amendments put off the deadlines for meeting air quality standards, especially those for automobile exhaust, until 1983.

In heavily polluted regions such as the South Coast Air Basin the deadlines were put even further off to 1987.

As the overseer of local air pollution regulation, it would fall to the ARB to become the nemesis of the Los Angeles APCD and, later, SCAQMD. When he was elected Governor in 1974 Jerry Brown appointed his campaign manager Tom Quinn as chairperson of the ARB. Quinn took an aggressive approach to the oversight function—especially as this applied to air pollution control in Southern California. Quinn led the challenge on all fronts: he challenged the scientific competence of the technical staff, the practices of the District enforcement personnel and the commitment of the administrative staff to clean air.[61]

A friendlier Governor, George Deukmajian has placed far less pressure on SCAQMD to perform. However, in the interim many of the citizen activists who had been critical of the Los Angeles APCD and of SCAQMD became members of the SCAQMD Board of Directors as state appointees and as alternates to the representatives of environmentally sensitive jurisdictions.

THE DEMAND FOR CLEAN AIR

From its first appearance, Southern California's smog has attracted considerable and sustained attention by citizen activists. Two forms of activism have characterized the demand for clean air in Southern California: political action specific to an event or incident; and sustained activity by ongoing political organizations. One of the characteristic features of air quality activism has been the increasing technical and political sophistication of the activists.

The history of this demand for clean air can be divided roughly into two periods: a period after the creation of the Los Angeles APCD when activists provided basic political support to the District and its actions; and a period beginning in the late 1960s when activists, with the maturation of the environmental movement, treated the District as part of the problem rather than as a champion of the cure. The demand function for clean air shifted dramatically upward. However, in the formative years of air pollution control, elite activism dominated the political agenda.

A prime mover in the creation of the County Smoke and Fumes Commission was the Altadena Property Owner's League. The League had been revived in July, 1944 by property owners in the Pasadena area to deal specifically with the air pollution problem. The League made a demand for "immediate enactment of a simple ordinance without further delays speciously justified by appeals to the need for more definitive scientific knowledge."[62]   To support this position, the League organized letter writing and petition drives that involved a wide range of organizations:

> The Supervisors, the Los Angeles City Council, the All-Year-Club, various little taxpayers' associations, and real estate and insurance firms received calls for the mobilization of the community. Few potential allies were overlooked as even the Public Health Service, the War Production Board, and the FBI received copies of the lament.[63]

In 1945 a Citizen's Fumes Committee took up where the Altadena Property Owners League had left off. The Committee spent much of 1945 decrying the air pollution problem to local officials and other community groups. The City Councils of sixteen neighboring communities responded to the call by the end of 1945. By the fall of 1946 the Pasadena Chamber of Commerce became actively involved in lobbying for more effective air pollution control.[64]

In the spring of 1946 the owner of the Huntington Hotel in Pasadena, Stephen Royce, became actively involved in the air pollution issue—going so far as to hire his own investigator at $500 per month. He played the facilitator, using his extensive business contacts and influence to bring together various interests and subdue opposition that was needed to create the State Legislation that would enable the creation of the Los Angeles Air Pollution Control District: it had been Royce who had involved Norman Chandler and the *Times* in the threat to give railroad and lumber companies a bad press. When the controversy over the Haagen-Smit discoveries emerged in 1951, it was

Royce who brought industry leaders together to act amicably on the problem.

In 1955 the Citizen's Anti-Smog Advisory Committee was the leading advocacy group in Los Angeles. That role was considerably diminished when the committee became embroiled with then "smog sheriff" Louis Fuller over the release of emissions data—a battle the Committee lost.

By the 1950s, a group of concerned parents became active in the air pollution issue forming "Stamp Out Smog" (SOS).[65] SOS would be the primary citizen activist group into the early 1970s. Structurally SOS was an organization of organizations, so that by 1968 it had 475 member organizations. Its basic political strategy was to work with the Los Angeles APCD staff while at the same time pressuring the Board of Supervisors to take effective action. SOS was intimately involved with the lobbying efforts at both the state and federal level to create the ARB and the Clean Air Act and its 1970 amendments.

In 1969 SOS broke with its long-standing support of the Los Angeles APCD over a regulation to control the emission of nitrogen oxides by stationary sources. At a hearing a leader of SOS decried the decrepitude of the Los Angeles APCD administrative staff under the leadership of Louis Fuller for its technical backwardness, unresponsiveness to calls for action and failure at adequate enforcement.[66]

The rise of the environmental professions and particularly the creation of air pollution research staffs at local universities supported the challenge being posed by citizens. For example, in the early 1970s CalTech was proposing alternative air pollution control plans, and the Statewide Air Pollution Research Laboratory at the University of California Riverside was questioning basic air pollution claims by the Los Angeles APCD.[67]

Clean Air Now, the Coalition for Clean Air, the Southern California Lung Association and the Sierra Club all became activist organizations involved with the air pollution issue in the 1970s. These groups shared the view that the Los Angeles APCD and SCAQMD are characterized by two features: first, the dominance of the technical fix as the regulatory method of choice; and second, both agencies had a pronounced willingness to accommodate the forces that promote decentralized economic growth in Southern California.

THE POLITICAL ECONOMY OF SOUTHERN CALIFORNIA

The 1920s saw an influx of immigrants, unmatched either before or since, into Southern California. This influx created the largest land boom in the history of a region famous for its land booms and real estate industry in general. The lure in the '20s had little to do with stampeding growth in manufacturing. The major industrial development in the '20s was in the wholesale and retail trades, with Los Angeles becoming a regional distribution center. In conjunction with this trade-based economy, Los Angeles surpassed San Francisco as the West Coast's leading port. It is important in this context to note that Los Angeles County continued throughout the 1940s to be first in the nation in agriculture-based wealth and income.[68]

It was not until the 1930s, and another although the less dramatic immigration, that the industries that would dominate Southern California burgeoned: rubber, apparel, oil, motion pictures and aircraft. This industrial and, particularly, manufacturing influx was preceded by six significant developments: first, the creation of an open-shop economy; second, the development of Los Angeles as a regional center; third, the development of infrastructural institutions such as the Metropolitan Water District and the City Planning Commission; fourth, the annexation by the city of outlying communities; fifth, the take-over of one of the two major electric rail systems; and sixth, a series of far-reaching plans for an extensive transportation network.[69] A central and important feature to this industrial base was that much of the new industry was export-based. Even the real estate industry was largely financed through East Coast banks up through the 1960s.[70]

World War II brought an expansion in population, especially Southern blacks, searching for manufacturing employment in defense industries. With this influx came yet another wave of decentralization—a pattern already established by the intra-war development of Southern California. However, the defense industries would remain as the mainstay of the economy of Southern California through the 1950s.[71] Of particular importance to the maturation of its economy was the location of branches of national corporations in Southern California, expanding the economic base beyond a regional focus.

Southern California's economic base, particularly its manufacturing sector, expanded and diversified throughout the 1960s. Defense-based industries shifted from airframe construction to electronics. Los Angeles matured into the preeminent financial center of the Pacific Rim. And employment growth in the region was led by non-defense manufacturing.[72] Among durable goods, manufacturing, machinery, electrical machinery, primary and fabricated metals, and transportation equipment, together, grew 65% and accounted for 45% of total manufacturing employment growth. Among non-durable goods, apparel grew 60% and accounted for 12% of total manufacturing employment growth.

The pattern of growth continued the theme of decentralization into the 1970s.[73] Employment growth centered in three areas: Burbank and Van Nuys at the southern edge of the San Fernando valley; the area surrounding the Los Angeles International Airport; and the border region of Los Angeles and Orange Counties, in the area from Long Beach to Anaheim. Population growth occurred in the communities adjacent to these regions.

During the 1970s the economic base continued to lose ground in transportation equipment but maintained the process of diversification in the other industries.[74] By the late 1970s and early 1980s the electronics industries were expanding further south into Orange County and light manufacturing industries were expanding north and west into the San Fernando valley and east into the San Gabriel and Pomona valleys.

Attendant upon this industrial growth was the transportation system that served it—the freeway that has become the hallmark of Los Angeles.[75] By the end of World War II the extensive electric trolley system[76] had been scrapped for a transportation system based on the private automobile. Although alleged to have been the victim of a conspiracy, the electric rail system was more a victim of Southern California's decentralization and the consequent incentives such a process created for a decentralized transportation system.

The first few miles of the Los Angeles freeway system were constructed in 1940; in 1953 Southern California had approximately 30 miles of freeway; by 1973 there were over 650 miles of freeway, and the milage increased modestly to a little over 700 miles by 1980.[77] These miles of asphalt began in the 1940s as short passageways intended to ease congestion. By 1960 major arteries were constructed from downtown Los Angeles north into the San Fernando valley, east into the San Gabriel and Pomona valleys, south to the Los Angeles and Long Beach harbors and southeast through Orange County. The end of the expansion in the early 1970s was marked by a spider's web of freeway systems enveloping the core regions from the San Fernando valley down through the northern half of Orange County.

Frederic Jaher marks the emergence of Los Angeles' contemporary elite with the end of World War I.[78] During the period between World War I and World War II the economic and superstructural basis for the subsequent development of Los Angeles' political economy was created. Southern California's elite was intimately involved in this process.

The intra-War superstructural institutions mentioned in the previous section all share the characteristic that they owe their existence primarily to the aegis of elite business organizations, such as the Merchants and Manufacturers Associations, the All Year Club, the Property Owner's Tax Association, the Downtown Businessmen's Association and, of course, the Chamber of Commerce. Frequently, these superstructural institutions also owed their governance to these elites as well—for example, the Metropolitan Water District and, of special interest, the Planning Commission.[79]

As would be expected, the economic base of the elite during the intra-War years was in the professions and trades—corresponding to the dominant industries in the region.[80] With World War II and the shift to a mature economic base having primary growth in manufacturing, the composition of the elite shifted into these industries.

Martin Schiesl remarks that "few cities matched Los Angeles' wartime concern with postwar urbanization."[81] Independently-funded organizations such as the Haynes Foundation, and even more relevant, the Southern California Air Pollution Foundation focused a considerable amount of energy and resources on developmental planning. Schiesl notes that one of the primary characteristics of post-War planning consisted of consortia of business organizations and professional planners. Indeed, the creation of the professionally staffed planning departments that were to perform in the post-War era were created by or at the very least at the instigation of elite organizations.

Later organizations such as the Southern California Association of Governments would be forced on Southern California rather than being created to serve some planning need.[82] However, the functioning of these institutions would continue in the mode of those institutions created at the beginning of the post-War era: the coordination of superstructural institutions to abet the privately planned development of Southern California and to abate the effects of the resulting political economy.

The historical account of planning institutions of Siminoski and Schiesl led them to conclude that the central actors performing the real planning function in post-War Los Angeles were the business elites with a peripheral role played by professional planners.[83] This conclusion also led them to focus on the exclusion of the converse: that is, greater citizen participation in the planning process. Another issue of even greater interest to these researchers was the extent to which neither the elite nor planners were complete masters of the destiny of Southern California.

Certainly a major focal point was the basic decentralization of the Southern California pattern of growth. Many critics focus on what are actually effects of decentralization, in particular the resistance of the business elite to support the funding of centralized infrastructures.[84] The central question is what incentives would the business elite, as a whole, have for creating such centralized infrastructures and superstructures? The answer is that the elite was divided at best: on one level, much of the decentralized transportation system was created by land developers specifically to get people out to their developments; and, on the other and most important level, there were no economic incentives during the formative intra-War years to create centralized infrastructures because there was no dominant centralized economic base.

SUMMARY AND CONCLUSION

The first and second dimensions of power apply easily to the account given of the supply and demand for clean air. In the first dimension, visible conflicts of interest appeared throughout: conflict between the two Smoke and Fumes Commissions over the form of pre-APCD regulation; conflict between APCD and industry scientists over the causes of smog; conflict between, on the one side, citizen activists and, on the other side, industry and pro-growth activists over specific regulatory issues and standards; conflict between local agencies on the one side and state and federal agencies on the other side over the implementation of the Clean Air Act; and, finally, conflict between local and state politicians preceding the creation of SCAQMD. The resolution of each of these conflicts has two characteristics that lend themselves to a supply/demand framework: all were subjected to intensive bargaining culminating in compromise resolutions; and over the long run these equilibria moved in the direction of more extensive regulation (i.e., exfoliation).

In the second dimension, conflicts were prevented from reaching a public forum. The enabling legislation that created both pre-APCD regulations and enabled creation of APCDs was constructed by the District Attorney with the active participation of the Chamber of Commerce. The success of the APCD enabling legislation and early APCD regulatory activity depended heavily on the intercession of business elite members such as Norman Chandler. Later efforts by the state to reform Los Angeles County air pollution regulation were derailed or postponed by local politicians.[85] And from a more structural standpoint, second degree power appeared as an enforcement philosophy oriented toward industry cooperation and the protracted delays in dealing with the automobile.

Although the second degree of power applies to the avoidance of public conflict, it fits into a supply/demand framework; much of the behind the scenes activity was in fact bargaining among the elite. As citizen activists became more sophisticated politically as well as technically, they too became involved in determining what issues made it to the public agenda. The most obvious manifestation of this has been the inclusion of activists such as Judy Orttung, Gladys Meade and Sabrina Schiller on the Board of Directors of SCAQMD: a move from outside bargaining to inside bargaining.

The second degree of power appears prominently in the broader history of the political economy of Southern California. Business elite organizations were intimately involved in shaping the institutions and institutionalized goals of the political economy of Southern California. Some of the same or similar business organizations, notably the

Chamber of Commerce, the Haynes Foundation, the All Year Club, and the Southern California Air Pollution Foundation, played a role in shaping both planning and air quality agencies and promoting developmental schemes. Most importantly, these organizations played a role in failing to realize planning goals such as effective mass transit because of unreconcilable differences among members of the elite. These facts play an important part in distinguishing the utilitarian, supply/demand model from the functionalist model.

The key concept for the functionalist model is hegemonic power. In the case of administrative personnel who implement policy, hegemonic power manifests itself as the desirable logic of cooperation with polluters in enforcing standards combined with the self-perception as objective technical experts. One source of this hegemonic power is the professionally transmitted ideology that is pro-growth and that defines pollution problems as engineering problems. In the case of the politicians who legislate air pollution policy, hegemonic power takes the form of political entrepreneurship in taking up the cause of environmental issues and subsequently subjecting them to the compromise of the legislative process. Hegemonic power also appears as the political risk minimizing behavior described earlier as exfoliation. In the case of activists, hegemonic power appears as the frequently unarticulated desire to incorporate environmental with economic decisionmaking. In order for activists to be effective, they must work to move policy and implementation in the right direction. In the case of the individual polluter, especially the automobile driver, hegemonic power is the lack of choice in transportation, other infrastructural and employment alternatives. In the case of the industrial polluter, hegemonic power appears as the anarchy of capitalist production,[86] the anarchy that "gives" the economy—the economic environment which all the other actors take as a given.

The ecological analogy brings to the fore the functionalist model. The individual pieces—the administrative apparatus, the political elite, the citizen activists—fit together to form a stable system. If a piece is disturbed or rearranged, then the other parts will move to re-establish the pre-existing arrangements. This is because the niche is defined by its interrelationships, not by its inherent characteristics. Indeed, the functionalist model accounts for system adjustments as the system calling forth the niche occupant with the correct characteristics.

A prime example is the appearance of successful chief administrators for air pollution control agencies. Both Smith Griswold and Jeb Stuart were successful because despite, or perhaps even because of their technical weakness, they were skilled bureaucratic politicians. The salient point is that these men were not selected for these skills. They were both selected in a time of crisis, after political legislators had followed the ideology of regulation and appointed technical people to the regulatory agency. In the same vein, the statement by the Riverside Grand Jury is particularly poignant: for example, despite Jeb Stuart's origins in a "victim" county, the circumstances surrounding both his appointment and his subsequent performance systematically mitigates against effective enforcement.

Oddly enough, incrementalism is a dominant feature of both the utilitarian and functionalist model. The focus, however, is quite different. The functionalist model postulates incremental change for the system as a whole; the utilitarian model postulates incremental change within a market. Stability in both models is based on the stability of the rules of the game: in the functionalist model it is the stability of the political economy of Southern California as a whole; for the utilitarian model it is the stability of the individual market. But in the two models the meaning of incrementalism and stability is radically different: the utilitarian model allows for a new stability when the rules change for a given market; the functionalist model incorporates incrementalism as a means of maintaining an over-arching stability despite nominal changes in the rules at the individual market level.

NOTES

1. A reference by Brodsly [71:1981] to the predominantly mid-western origins of immigrants to Southern California in the late nineteenth and early twentieth century.

2. The technical information in this section is taken from Lynn [1976], Keith [1980] and Keith [1964].

3. A normal temperature gradient in the atmosphere is characterized by an inverse relationship between ambient air temperature and height: as elevation increases, temperature falls. An inversion layer literally inverts the normal gradient so that temperature rises with elevation. With the normal gradient, a mass of air at the Earth's surface will rise since it is warmer than the air surrounding it at each elevation. When that air mass (and most importantly the effluents carried in it) reaches an inversion layer it is no warmer than the ambient air and hence ceases to rise. The inversion layer itself is created in the South Coast Air Basin when the cool, moist marine system that stands over the Pacific Ocean is overlaid by the warm, dry air system that stands over the continental United States. When this latter continental system is sufficiently strong it pushes the marine layer literally out to sea, creating the so-called Santa Ana conditions. When the Pacific system is strong relative to the continental system, the inversions disappear.

4. Chemical compounds consisting of at least of hydrogen and carbon atoms. Methane (what is burned in home gas appliances) with one carbon atom and four hydrogen atoms is a hydrocarbon, but not a reactive one. Generally the most reactive hydrocarbons have from four to ten carbon atoms--gasoline is, as the octane rating suggests, dominated by eight carbon atom compounds.

5. This has not excluded other processes that put pollutants or pollutant precursors into the air. Evaporation is probably the other major process. For example, the vapor recovery devices on

gas pump nozzles are used to capture the gasoline vapor that would otherwise escape when displaced by gasoline pumped into the tank of motor vehicles. Another evaporative source of reactive hydrocarbons is the use of petroleum based paints—especially the enamels used in automobile painting and body work. I note the irony that the use of the automobile has created at least two stationary air pollution sources.

6.   Technically referred to as suspended particulates. It is worth noting that the "smoking" automobile is producing suspended particulates, not smog.

7.   These include sources as varied steel mills and backyard incinerators.

8.   There is a peculiarity that makes the extrapolation from low nitrogen oxides and hydrocarbons to low ozone a tricky one. There is a direct relationship between the formation of photochemical oxidants and the concentration of hydrocarbons. However, for any given concentration of hydrocarbon there will be a concentration of nitrogen oxides at which the concentration of oxidant formed will peak. As a consequence it is possible to *decrease* the concentration of photochemical oxidant formed by *increasing* the concentration of nitrogen oxide emissions.

9.   In contrast to motor vehicles, stationary sources are virtually always in "cruise"—where hydrocarbon and nitrogen oxide production result in relatively low ozone production.

10. DeVoss [1986].

11. Los Angeles *Times* [1987A].

12. And, as an ultimate irony, the study had to be postponed because Southern California experienced an exceptionally clement period during the week when the study was to take place—of all things, Los Angeles could not deliver on its much heralded smog. Los Angeles *Times* [1987B].

13. Upon landing at San Pedro Bay, Cabrillo named the Los Angeles basin La Bahia de Los Fumos—the Bay of Smokes. Krier and Ursin [45:1977].

14. Brienes [1976] and [1975].

15. Brienes [35:1975].

16. Los Angeles had become second only to Akron, Ohio in the production of synthetic rubber, largely as a result of a locational decision made by native-son William Jeffers as administrator of the Rubber Reserve Corporation.

17. Los Angeles *Times* [1943A].

18. One Commissioner would later observe that the Commission had been convened in order to "take the pressure off the Supervisors for the butadiene plant problem." Brienes [60:1975].

19. Brienes [74:1975].

20. Brienes [76:1975].

21. Both quotes cited in Brienes [77:1975].

22. Brienes [90:1975].

23. Brienes [91:1975].

24. Brienes [91:1975].

25. Krier and Ursin [55-56:1977].

26. Krier and Ursin [56:1977].

27. Brienes [98:1975].

28. On air pollution specifically see Grinder [1980] and [1978]. For the pervasiveness of this educate-and-persuade approach see Schultz and McShane [1980].

29. Brienes [99:1975].

30. It is extremely important to emphasize at this point that the Los Angeles County APCD and the Los Angeles County Board of Supervisors were the same body of people. In the writing on the subject there is a somewhat unnerving tendency to talk as if the APCD were only the administrative apparatus that served as staff to the Board. Hopefully, such lapses are not encountered here.

31. Mr. McCabe's selection also made sense because his application for the position had been solicited by County Administrative Office Wayne Allen. Mr. Allen had worked with Mr. McCabe during World War II on coal production in Belgium. The Meuse Valley in Belgium was the site of one the first highly publicized air pollution disasters in the twentieth century: the disaster occurred in 1930 and killed several hundred people.

32. Brienes [171:1976].

33. In fact, the Foundation was another research vehicle for the oil industry, with WOGA contributing approximately $1 million of the $3 million it spent before its dissolution in 1960.

34. Dorn had run unopposed, but had made the air pollution issue a major part of his platform. Dorn's former occupation had been TV newscaster. Doty [71-73:1978].

35. The senior staff of the APCD openly supported Dorn.

36. The attorney who handled the suit, Mary Nichols, would later be appoint chair of the California Air Resources Board by Governor Jerry Brown.

37. Doty [179:1978].

38.   Zafman [1972]; Haagen-Smit [1973].

39.   The man who had been hired way from the Los Angeles Police
      Department Motorcycle Patrol in the 1950s to become the
      APCDs smog "sheriff", responsible for nabbing polluters in the
      act.

40.   In fact, Chass had been an assistant to Gordon Larson.

41.   AB #250. Amendment to California Health and Safety Code
      Chapter 324.

42.   AB 2883.

43.   Los Angeles *Times* [1976A].

44.   Los Angeles *Times* [1974A]. Birakos held the same position with
      the SCAQMD. It is doubtful that he intended his remarks to be
      ironic.

45.   This concern with "home rule" by the Southern California
      counties was not confined to air pollution regulation. The same
      counties (with the addition of Imperial County) had effectively
      resisted the empowerment of the Southern California Association
      of Governments in the late 1960s. This regional agency, formed
      under state and national legislation mandating action in the
      formation of local and regional Council of Governments (COGs),
      while nominally a regional planning agency, was restricted in its
      enabling legislation to an advisory role only. The formation of
      the Southern California Association of Governments (SCAG)
      took place under circumstances not dissimilar to the formation
      of the Southern California APCD--namely, under the threat of
      State legislation that would have created a genuine regional
      planning agency. Johnson [1976].

46.   Los Angeles *Times* [1975].

47. The only steel mill on the West Coast. The now retired mill, built during World War II, was the premier polluter in the eastern end of the South Coast Air Basin.

48. Riverside (California) *Press-Enterprise* [1974B].

49. Riverside (California) Grand Jury [1975:5].

50. Riverside (California) *Press-Enterprise* [1974A].

51. *LA Weekly* [1980:12]. As a matter of law, court rulings handed down in the early 1970s *do* require that cost be ignored when considering how to achieve the provisions of the Clean Air Act.

52. Los Angeles *Times* [1987B].

53. Mandelker and Rothschild [1973], Downing and Brady [1978], Hays [1980].

54. Krier and Ursin [284:1977].

55. Krier and Ursin [137-169:1977].

56. Simmons and Cutting [1974].

57. This was the same consortium that began with a lengthy and heated correspondence between the auto makers, the Automobile Manufacturer's Association and Supervisor Hahn back in the late 1950s. Krier and Ursin [87-88:1977].

58. Simmons and Cutting [1974].

59. Chernow [1975].

60. Hays [1980].

61. Doty [124-129:1978].

62.   Brienes [69:1975].

63.   Brienes [70:1975].

64.   This reflected a change in strategy by the Chamber based on a concern with the ability of Pasadena to maintain its attractions as a tourist center and residential suburban oasis.

65.   Kavaler [1968].

66.   Doty [89-94:1978].

67.   Greenburg [1976].

68.   Jaher [659-670:1982]; Brodsly [70-85:1981].

69.   Including a subway system. Jaher [659-679:1982]; Brodsly [80-96:1981].

70.   Jaher [661-2:1982].

71.   Clayton [1962].

72.   Soja, Morales and Wolff [1983].

73.   Preston [1972].

74.   Soja, Morales and Wolff [1983].

75.   Brodsly [1981].

76.   A system which at its height in the 1940s had the most miles of track of any urban system in existence. Brodsly [82:1981].

77.   Brodsly [120-130:1981].

78.   Jaher [577-709:1982].

79. Jaher [658-663:1982].

80. Jaher [665-670:1982].

81. Schiesl [130:1980].

82. Johnson [1976].

83. Siminoski [1978].

84. Whitt [1982].

85. Peter Shabarum and Kenneth Hahn in particular.

86. The anarchy is in the selectivity of planning, not in the lack of planning.

REFERENCES

Allison, Oscar Hugh. 1978. Raymond R. Tucker: the smoke elimination years, 1934-1950. Ph.D. Dissertation, St. Louis University.

Boyarsky, Bill and Boyarsky, Nancy. 1974. *Backroom politics: how your local politicians work, why your government doesn't and what you can do about it.* Los Angeles: J.P. Torcher.

Brienes, Marvin. 1976. Smog comes to Los Angeles. *Historical Society of Southern California.* 58:4 (Winter, 1976), 515-532.

Brienes, Marvin. 1975. The fight against smog in Los Angeles, 1943-1957. Ph.D. Dissertation, University of California, Davis.

Brodsly, David. 1981. *LA freeway: an appreciative essay.* Berkeley: University of California.

Chass, Robert and Feldman, Edward S. 1954. Tears for John Doe. *Southern California law review.* 27 (1954), 349-372.

Chernow, Eli. 1975. Implementing the Clean Air Act in Los Angeles: the duty to achieve the impossible. *Ecology law quarterly.* 4 (1975), 537-581.

Clayton, James L. 1962. Defense spending: key to California's growth. *The western political quarterly.* (June, 1962), 280-293.

Congressional Quarterly. 1982. *Regulation: process and politics.* Washington, DC: Congressional Quarterly.

Connick, Nancy, et al. 1971. Smog: a paradox. Program in public policy studies of the Claremont College. (April, 1971).

Cottrell, Edwin A. and Jones, Helen L. 1952. *Characteristics of the metropolis.* Los Angeles: The Haynes Foundation.

DeVoss, David. 1986. New strategies against an old enemy. *Los Angeles Times Magazine*. (July 20, 1986), 17-22.

Doty, Robert Adam. 1978. Life cycle theories of regulatory agency behavior: the Los Angeles Air Pollution Control District. Ph.D. Dissertation, University of California, Riverside.

Downing, Paul B. and Brady, Gordon. 1978. Implementing the Clean Air Act: a case study of oxidant control in Los Angeles. *Natural resources journal*. 18 (April, 1978), 237-283.

Englebert, Ernest A. 1954. *Planning for the economic growth of Southern California*. Berkeley: University of California Extension.

Espisito, John C. 1970. *Vanishing air*. New York: Grossman.

Fogelson, Robert M. 1967. *The fragmented metropolis: Los Angeles, 1850-1930*. Cambridge, MA: Harvard.

Greenburg, William. 1976. Smog and politics in Los Angeles. *Sierra*. (June, 1976), 22-25.

Grinder, Dale R. 1980. *Pollution and reform in American cities, 1870-1930*. Austin: University of Texas.

Grinder, Dale R. 1978. From insurgency to efficiency: the smoke abatement campaign in Pittsburgh before World War I. *The western Pennsylvania historical magazine*. 61:3 (July, 1978), 187-202.

Haagen-Smit, Arie. 1973. Final report: investigation of the Los Angeles Air Pollution Control District. (January 3, 1973).

Hagevik, George H. 1970. *Decision-making in air pollution control: a review of theory and practice, with emphasis on selected Los Angeles and New York City management experiences*. New York: Praeger.

Hays, Samuel P. 1980. The structure of environmental politics since World War II. *Journal of social history*. 14:1 (1980), 719-738.

Hirsch, Werner ed. 1971. *Los Angeles: viability and prospects for metropolitan leadership*. New York: Praeger.

Hohm, Charles F. 1976. A human-ecological approach to the reality and perception of air pollution: the Los Angeles case. *Pacific sociological review*. 19:1 (January, 1976), 21-44.

Ingram, Helen. 1978. The political rationality of innovation: the Clean Air Act Amendments of 1970. Ann Friedlaender, ed. *Approaches to controlling air pollution*. Cambridge, MA: MIT, 1978. 12-56.

Jaher, Frederic Cople. 1982. *The urban establishment: upper strata in Boston, New York, Charleston, Chicago, and Los Angeles*. Urbana, Illinois: University of Illinois.

Johnson, Joke. 1976. The Southern California Association of Governments. Ph.D. Dissertation, Clairemont College.

Jones, Charles O. 1974. Federal-state-local sharing in air pollution control. *Publius: the journal of federalism*. 4:1 (Winter, 1974), 69-88.

Krier, James E. and Ursin, Edmund. 1977. *Pollution and policy: a case essay on California and Federal experience with motor vehicle pollution control, 1940-1975*. Berkeley:University of California, 1977.

Kavaler, Lucy. 1968. How Los Angeles women are fighting smog--and winning. *Redbook*. (September, 1968), 55, 99-100.

Kennedy, Harold and Porter, Andrew. 1955. Air pollution: its control and abatement. *Vanderbilt law review*. 8 (1955), 854-877.

Kidner, Frank L. and Neff, Phillip. 1945. *An economic survey of the Los Angeles Area*. Los Angeles: The Haynes Foundation.

LA Weekly. 1986. Duke loves smog. (August 8, 1986), 8.

LA Weekly. 1980. LA's smog control agency: who's in control? 2:46 (October 23, 1980), 15-21.

Lamare, Judith. 1973. Urban mass transportation politics in the Los Angeles area. Ph.D. Dissertation, University of California, Los Angeles.

Los Angeles *Times*. 1987A. 200 experts to pick apart Southland air in smog study. Part I (June 1, 1987), 3.

Los Angeles *Times*. 1987B. AQMD Board to fight reorganization move. Part I (June 6, 1987), 10.

Los Angeles *Times*. 1982. L.A. mass transit: it's a slow and agonizing procedure. Part IV (May 16, 1982), 1,7-11.

Los Angeles *Times*. 1976A. Brown signs bill for new Southland smog agency. Part I (July 3, 1976), 1.

Los Angeles *Times*. 1976B. Legislature OKs new Southland pollution board. Part I (September 26, 1976), 1.

Los Angeles *Times*. 1975. Letter to the editor by Robert Lunche. Part I (July 11, 1975), 4.

Los Angeles *Times*. 1974A. Veto of smog measure will bring tougher plan in '75, Backers Say. Part I (September 28, 1974), 18.

Los Angeles *Times*. 1974B. Reagan vetoes bills on smog district change and marijuana. Part I (September 28, 1974), 1.

Los Angeles *Times*. 1973A. Moretti plans bill to stiffen smog control, Replace APCD. Part I (July 4, 1973), 3.

Los Angeles *Times*. 1973B. Assembly OKs 4 bills to step up smog fight. Part I (August 8, 1973), 3.

Los Angeles *Times*. 1947A. Times expert offers smog plan. Part I (January 19, 1947), 1.

Los Angeles *Times*. 1947B. Text of report and conclusions of smog expert. Part I (January 19, 1947), 1.

Los Angeles *Times*. 1943A. Butadiene plant confirmed as source of gas fumes here. Part I (July 29, 1943), 1.

Los Angeles *Times*. 1943B. Industry blamed for 'gas attack'. Part II (July 26, 1943), 3.

Lynn, David A. 1976. *Air pollution: threat and response*. Reading, MA: Addison-Wesley.

Mandelker, Daniel R. and Rothschild, Susan B. 1973. The role of land-use controls in combatting air pollution under the Clean Air Act of 1970. *Ecology law quarterly*. 3:2 (Spring, 1973), 235-375.

Melosi, Martin V. ed. 1980. *Pollution and reform in American cities, 1870-1930*. Austin: University of Texas.

Preston, Richard E. 1972. The changing form and structure of the Southern California metropolis—part II. *The California geographer*. 8 (1972), 33-47.

Preston, Richard E. 1971. The changing form and structure of the Southern California metropolis--part I. *The California geographer*. 7 (1971), 5-20.

Quarles, John. 1977. The transportation control plans—federal regulation's collision with reality. *Harvard environmental law review*. 2 (1977), 241-263.

Riverside (California) Grand Jury. 1974. *1973-74 Riverside County Grand Jury Report, Attachment A.*

Riverside *Press-Enterprise*. 1976. Governor creates new Southland smog district. Part B (July 3, 1976), 1.

Riverside *Press-Enterprise*. 1975. Riversider to lead new 4-county APCD. Part B (July 3, 1975), 1.

Riverside *Press-Enterprise*. 1974A. McCandless, Record met Kinley in secret before resignation. Part B (April 1, 1974), 1.

Riverside *Press-Enterprise*. 1974B. Grand Jury probes APCD operations. Part B (March 20, 1974), 1.

Riverside *Press-Enterprise*. 1974C. Pollution officer says management key to his job. Part B (June 15, 1974), 1.

Riverside *Press-Enterprise*. 1973. Problems develop within air pollution control unit. Part B (May 13, 1973), 1.

Riverside *Press-Enterprise*. 1970. Pollution control chief to leave post next week. Part B (March 6, 1970), 1.

Roberts, Thomas Raymond. 1969. Motor vehicle air pollution control in California: a case of political unresponsiveness. Honors Thesis, Harvard.

Schiesl, Martin J. 1980. City planning and the federal government in World War II: the Los Angeles experience. *California history*. 19:2 (Summer, 1980), 126-143.

Schultz, Stanley K. and McShane, Clay. 1980. Pollution and political reform in urban America: the role of the municipal engineer. Melosi, Martin V, *Pollution and reform in American cities, 1870-1930.* Austin: University of Texas, 1980. 155-172.

Siminoski, Dan. 1978. The myth of comprehensive urban planning: a critical study of the development of the Los Angeles General Plan. Ph.D. Dissertation, University of Wisconsin, Madison.

Simmons, William and Cutting, Robert H., Jr. 1974. A many layered wonder: non-vehicular air pollution control law in California. *The Hastings law journal.* 26 (September, 1974), 109-166.

Sims, Harold Lahn. 1973. The emergence of air pollution as a political issue in Southern California, 1940-1970. Ph.D. Dissertation, University of California, Riverside.

Soja, Edward, Morales, Rebecca and Wolff, Goetz. 1983. Urban restructuring: an analysis of social and spatial change in Los Angeles. *Economic geography*. 59:2 (April, 1983), 195-230.

Trankly, Lisa. 1979. Stationary source air pollution control in California: a proposed jurisdictional reorganization. *UCLA law review*. 26 (1979), 893-924.

Whitt, J. Allen. 1982. *Urban elites and mass transportation: the dialectics of power*. Princeton: Princeton University.

Willick, Daniel H. and Windle, Timothy J. 1973. Rule enforcement by the Los Angeles County Air Pollution Control District. *Ecology law quarterly*. 3 (1973), 507-534.

Wilson, James Q. 1967. A guide to Reagan country: the political culture of Southern California. *Commentary*. 43:5 (May, 1967), 37-45.

Wilson, Jane. 1972. Scenario for a smog snafu. *Los Angeles* Times *West Magazine*. (January 9, 1972), 1.

Zafman, Norman. 1972. Profile of an air pollution controversy: the Air Resources Board investigates the Los Angeles Air Pollution Control District. *Beverly Hills Bar journal*. (September, 1972), 46-56.

CHAPTER 4

Air Quality

This chapter looks at what happened to air quality in Southern California over the last fifty years. Insofar as visibility reduction can be used as an indicator of air quality, the numbers indicate that air quality has improved. However, there is some indication that the improvement has been in a reduction of accute air quality problems: severe episodes of air pollution. Chronic air pollution—the persistent presence of air pollutants—has not particularly improved.

This suggests two things: first, that regulators were able to increasingly avoid severe conditions; but, second, they have only been able to keep pollutant reductions in pace with the growth of source activity.

The effectiveness of an institutional structure has a stable relationship with the environmental goods it affects. When institutional change occurs, the delivery of the environmental good changes. As the previous chapters have discussed, the meaning of "institutional change" has two interpretations. The utilitarian account pictures change as change in incentives; the functionalist account pictures change as change in the economic base.

AN AIR QUALITY INDICATOR

The first problem is how to measure air quality in a way that will allow for an analysis of institutional change. The major difficulty in finding such an indicator is that the systematic measurement of pollutants is a fairly recent development. One reason for the lack of adequate data is that measurement of air pollutants became of interest only after regulation began. A related, and even more important reason, is that many pollutants were either not identified or not even discovered until after regulation began. Yet another difficulty is that the ideal air quality indicator needs to have three important features in order to be usable: it must be a direct measure of air quality; it must have been measured consistently for the period of concern; and it must extend over the appropriate time period and geographic area.

First, the selected indicator must be a genuine, direct measure of air quality. "Genuine" means a measure which is itself not an index in the technical sense. An example of the latter kind of index is the South Coast Air Quality Management District's 500 point Pollutant Standards Index (PSI). "Direct" means a measure of an effluent or product of atmospheric chemistry, rather than a measure of an effect or perception of air pollution. An example of the latter kind of indicator is the log of complaints that air pollution agencies receive. Implied in this first criterion is the idea that the selected indicator must be the result of a process that regulators act on in a direct way.

Second, the selected indicator must be one that has been measured in a consistent, uniform way for the period covered. It is critical to ensure that there are neither discontinuities nor ambiguities in what is being measured. As the science of air pollution has developed, what should be measured and how to measure it have been both technically and politically contentious. In the history of air pollution control, both what to measure and how to measure it have been contentious issues.

The third and final characteristic of the ideal air quality indicator is that it must span the impact of regulatory institutions in both time and space. The selected indicator must span the time period preceding as well as that following the creation of regulatory institutions and the implementation of air pollution regulations.

The selected indicator must also have observations from locations throughout the South Coast Air Basin (SCAB). This feature is necessary because of the change in institutional structures that have taken place geographically among the jurisdictions within the SCAB.

The air quality indicator that most closely satisfies these criteria is the measurement of visibility reduction at various locations within the South Coast Air Basin. The following assays how visibility reduction meets these criteria.

First, visibility reduction as a direct measure of air quality has two weaknesses. The first weakness is that, although visibility has been an issue in air pollution control, visibility reduction has never been a primary air quality indicator (i.e., has never been itself something that air pollution control regulators have been required to abate in the way that, for instance, photochemical oxidant has been regulated). The second weakness is that visibility reduction is only one of a myriad of air quality indicators (whether directly requiring regulatory action or not). Furthermore visibility reduction itself is treated more as an aesthetic rather than as a health problem.[1]

However, although not itself considered a primary indicator of air quality, visibility reduction is systematically related to several of the major pollutants or with processes closely associated with these pollutant[2]: namely, sulphur dioxide[3], ozone[4], oxides of nitrogen[5] and hydrocarbons.[6]

The visual impact of smog is probably one of the primary and most immediate impacts that smog has on the citizens of Southern California. Ambient nitrogen dioxide (having a red-brown color) is alone among primary pollutants in being directly observable.[7] This is not to deny or diminish the fact that the health effects of the "invisible" primary pollutants have a far more profound economic effect than the aesthetics of the daily observation of whether the air looks "clean" or not. Thus, although other indicators may be more relevant both from a regulatory and health impact point of view, visibility has remained in the long term the primary form of air pollution experience in Southern California.

Secondly, visibility reduction is one among a few air quality indicators that have been measured using the same methodology throughout its history. These measurements are made by an agency—the Federal Aviation Administration (FAA)—that is not directly involved with air pollution control on any level. The data are collected for the purpose of monitoring air traffic safety. Observations that serve as the measure of visibility are collected at local airports by FAA personnel hourly. Objects at various distances and directions along the horizon are established as sighting objects. The average visibility is recorded as the distance to the furtherest of these designated objects that can be seen along 180° out of the 360° horizon.

Third and finally, the data on visibility reduction are extensively distributed over both time and geographic location. For this study, three observation set were used: a study of seven sites within the South Coast Air Quality Management District (SCAQMD); data for downtown Los Angeles maintained by SCAQMD; and a study conducted by the FAA.

VISIBILITY DATA SOURCES

The Los Angeles Air Pollution Control District and subsequently the South Coast Air Quality Management District (SCAQMD) collected FAA data and published several reports under the authorship of Ralph Keith, the chief meteorologist for these agencies.[8] These data are based on the minimum visibility reading made on a given day (all the hourly sightings made during normal daylight hours). The dependent variable used in these studies is the number of days when the minimum observation was less than three miles.[9]

Another study[10] conducted by Ralph Keith along with raw data from SCAQMD allowed a more extended and detailed data set for downtown Los Angeles. Three time series of visibility observations were created: the percent of days per year having minimum observations less than three miles, the percent of days per year having minimum observations less than seven miles and an annual average of minimum visibility observations.

As part of a larger study of airport visibility trends, the Federal Aviation Administration (FAA) conducted a study that included Los Angeles International Airport (LAX).[11] From these data two series were derived: the percent of all observations per year with visibility less than three miles and the percent of observations per year having observations less than seven miles.[12]

Detailed visibility reduction data was collected in downtown Los Angeles beginning in 1933. This data was recorded in a study by Keith[13] and updated with detailed data maintained by the SCAQMD.

The Keith SCAQMD studies are the most extensive in terms of geographic distribution, consisting of data from five[14] locations throughout the SCAB: Los Angeles International Airport; Burbank Municipal Airport; Long Beach Municipal Airport; Norton Air Force Base (San Bernardino); and March Air Force Base (Riverside). These locations are shown in Figure 4-1.

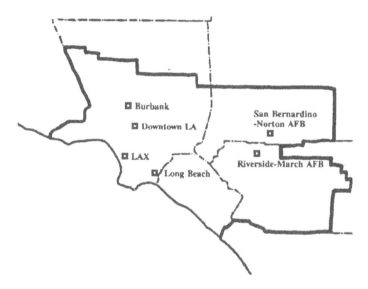

Figure 4-1
Locations in South Coast Air Basin of visibility reduction source data

Los Angeles International Airport (LAX) is on the Pacific Ocean west of downtown Los Angeles and in the vicinity of major oil refining activity to its south and a hub of light industrial development during the 1960s. The FAA study differs from the Keith SCAQMD studies in the detail of data recorded.

Burbank Municipal Airport is in the San Fernando Valley north of downtown Los Angeles—a site of major suburbanization after World War II. Long Beach Municipal Airport is to the south of downtown Los Angeles on the border of Los Angeles and Orange Counties—another site of suburbanization and more recently the location of industrial growth. Although Long Beach Airport is jurisdictionally in Los Angeles County, it is affected by Orange County activity and thus can act as a surrogate "location" within Orange County. Norton Air Force Base is located in San Bernardino on the eastern edge of the SCAB. It is both upwind from metropolitan Los Angeles and, more immediately, upwind from Kaiser Steel—the West Coast's only steel mill.[15] March Air Force Base is located just southeast of Riverside on the eastern edge of the SCAB. It is upwind of Orange County as well as metropolitan Los Angeles.[16]

The Keith studies cover the period 1950 to 1982. For Riverside, San Bernardino and Long Beach (as the surrogate for Orange County), this captures the period in which the Air Pollution Control Districts (APCDs) for their respective counties were created.

Data from Burbank and LAX, both of which were under the jurisdiction of the Los Angeles APCD, do not span the creation of this APCD. However, these data do span significant institutional changes in air pollution control within the Los Angeles jurisdiction.

The downtown Los Angeles data cover the period 1933 to 1979[17]—capturing not only the creation of the Los Angeles APCD but also the shift in the economy of Southern California marked by World War II. The FAA LAX Study data covers the period 1948 to 1978. Like the LAX data from the Keith Studies, these data do not span the creation of the Los Angeles APCD but do cover other periods of relevant institutional change.

THE TREND IN VISIBILITY REDUCTION

The twenty figures in Appendix A and Appendix B graph the visibility reduction data discussed above. Each set of data is shown twice with a linear (Appendix A) and a cubic (Appendix B) least squares estimator plotted through the data. The tables that follow the graphs in Appendix C list the data graphed. The econometric results of the linear and cubic models are given in Appendix D.

In the first group of ten graphs, the data for each location has a simple, least squares regression line plotted through it for the purpose of orientation: visibility reduction is the dependent variable regressed against the serial year.[18] The second group of graphs has a least squares line using a third degree polynomial[19] functional form for the model. The tables of the data appear in the same order as the figures.

In the first figures of each set of graphs (labelled "Average Daily Minimum Visibility, Downtown Los Angeles, 1933-1979") the variable plotted is an average. Improvements in air quality are therefore indicated when the average visibility increases: when the value of the variable increases and the slope of the regression is positive.

The remaining eighteen figures are of variables expressed as a percent. In the Keith SCAQMD studies, the variable is the percent of days when the minimum visibility reading was less than three miles. In the FAA study as well as the downtown Los Angeles studies, there are two variables. One variable is the percent of all observations having a reading less than three miles, while the other variable is the percent of all observations less than seven miles.

Improvements are therefore indicated when this percentage decreases: when the value of the variable decreases and the slope of the regression line is negative.

The single series from downtown Los Angeles that is of the average minimum visibility is a fairly broad gauge of air quality in that area of the SCAB. The less-than-three-miles variable at the various locations within the SCAB is an indicator of the frequency with which severe air pollution episodes occur. The less-than-seven-miles variable at downtown Los Angeles and at Los Angeles International Airport is an indicator of the persistence of chronic air pollution in the western portion of the SCAB.

In evaluating the results of the econometric tests applied to these data, five test were used: the Durbin-Watson statistic; F-statistic of restricted versus unrestricted models; the sense or direction of the coefficients; the significance of the independent variable; and the adjusted R^2 of the regression.

The Durbin-Watson statistic tests for autoregressive processes. Econometric results that make it possible to accept the hypothesis that autoregressive processes are not present are preferred to results that are indeterminate[20]; however, within any confidence interval (e.g., accept the hypothesis of non-autoregressive processes at 1% confidence) differences in the actual statistics are ignored and models are selected on other criteria; the minimum criterion of acceptability is indeterminacy at 1% confidence.

The F-statistic test one model against another to see if the addition of explanatory variables or a change in functional form improves the estimates. In this chapter, comparison is between the linear and cubic functional form (i.e., the addition of the square and cube of the independent variable to the model). In the next two chapters, the test is on variables added to the model to represent structural change. Models are rejected which show no significant improvement at the 10% confidence level.

The values for the coefficients of the regression need to make basic sense in terms of the story the independent variables tell about visibility reduction. This is especially true in the causal model presented in Chapter 6 where the basic requirement is that source activity be positively correlated with the worsening of visibility.

A standard t-statistic is used. The minimum acceptable value is for the coefficient to be significantly different from zero at a confidence of 80%. t-statistics less than this are treated as zero (indicated in the summary table with "No Change" followed by the direction of the coefficient).

An adjusted R^2 is used in two ways. The first application of this criterion is a simple ranking of results (i.e., being closely equivalent in other respects, which model has the greatest explanatory power). The second application of this statistic is the comparison of different functional forms of the estimators. In this chapter, the linear form is compared to the cubic form. In the next two chapter, models with and without structural change are compared to determine whether, based on an F-test, the improvement in explanatory power is statistically significant at a confidence level of 10%. The test used is[21]

$$F = \frac{R^2_{UR} - R^2_R}{1 - R^2_{UR}} \times \frac{N-k}{q}$$

where

R^2_{UR} = R^2 of the piecewise estimate
  = ratio of the explained to total variation of the regression with $k - 1$ coefficients

R^2_U = R^2 of the no-piece estimate
  = ratio of the explained to total variation of the regression restricted to $(k - q - 1)$ coefficients

N = number of observations

k = number of coefficients in the piecewise model

q = number of coefficients to create the cubic model (in this Chapter) or the structural change model (Chapters 5 and 6)

Based on the application of a linear model to the data, for the most part air quality has improved. Only the Riverside data and long-term (1933-1979) Downtown Los Angeles data show deteriorating air quality. The downtown Los Angeles series of chronic (i.e., less-than-seven-miles) air pollution shows no trend.

With the exception of the data from the FAA Study the Durbin-Watson statistics generally indicate autoregressive processes, implying that the Linear Functional Form has not captured the trend in air quality. These results are reinforced by the generally poor correlation coefficients of the regressions. However, with the exception of the Downtown Los Angeles Less Than 7 Miles series, the F-Statistics for all of the estimates are significant at the 10% level. Table 4-I summarizes results fully presented in Appendix D.

Table 4-I

Results of linear estimator applied to visibility data

Location and Dependent Variable	Air Quality Trend	Autoregressive Process?
Downtown LA (1933-1979)		
< 3 miles	Improve	No
< 7 miles	No Change (Improve)	Indeterminate
Average	Worsen	No
Los Angeles International Airport		
< 3 miles (Keith)	Improve	No
< 3 miles (FAA)	Improve	Yes
< 7 miles (FAA)	Improve	Yes
Burbank	Improve	No
Long Beach	Improve	No
Riverside	Worsen	Indeterminate
San Bernardino	Improve	No

In general, similar results are shown when a cubic (third degree polynomial) function is used instead of the linear function—with subtle differences. The use of the cubic function also generally shows an improvement in explanatory power, as would be expected. The heuristic difference between the two functional forms has to do primarily with the explanation of the processes underlying the time series and the trend that these processes cause. The linear function represents a constant trend corresponding to a constant improvement or deterioration in air quality—e.g., constant increments in institutional effectiveness at abatement. In contrast, the cubic function represents variable increments or decrements in effectiveness—e.g., institutions becoming more effective as time goes on.

The reading of the results of the estimates using a cubic function as the estimator are not as straightforward as those for the linear estimator. The "slope" of the estimate is the first derivative of the function—i.e., a quadratic function. Thus the "slope" or rate of change itself changes by year: the trend may show improvement for one period

Table 4-II

Comparison of cubic to linear estimator of visibility data

Location and Dependent Variable	Direction of Trends		Cubic Better Than Linear Model?	
	2nd Derivative	3rd Derivative	R^2	Autoregression
Downtown LA (1933-79)				
Average	Improve	Worsen	Yes	Yes
< 3 miles	No Change (Improve)	No Change (Worsen)	Yes	Yes
< 7 miles	Worsen	Improve	Yes	Yes
Los Angeles International Airport				
< 3 miles (Keith)	Improve	Worsen	Yes	Yes
< 3 miles (FAA)	No Change (Improve)	No Change (Worsen)	No	No Change
< 7 miles (FAA)	Improve	Worsen	No	No Change
Burbank	Worsen	Improve	Yes	Yes
Long Beach	No Change	No Change (Improve)	Yes (Improve)	Yes
Riverside	Worsen	Improve	Yes	Yes
San Bernardino	No Change (Improve)	No Change (Improve)	Yes	Yes

followed by deterioration in another depending on the second derivative. The second derivative of the cubic function is a linear function, and is also non-constant over the series: the second derivative will either tend to reinforce or counteract the trend represented by the first derivative; a trend that shifts from improvement to deterioration has a second derivative that shows deterioration. The third derivative is a constant. The third derivative can be interpreted as the rate at which changes in visibility reduction change.[22]

Technically the third derivative is the trend in the second derivative; the second derivative in turn is the trend in the first derivative; the first derivative is the trend of the data. However, there is a transitive relationship among these: a third derivative that indicates improvement translates into a second derivative that is changing toward improvement if it does not already indicate improvement; this in turn eventually leads to a first derivative that tends toward improvement. Consequently, the second derivative—although technically the rate of change of the trend—is interpreted as the trend. The third derivative is interpretted as the rate of change in the trend.

Table 4-II summarizes the results given in Appendix D comparing the cubic to the linear estimator and showing the superiority of the cubic model. Although the results paint a picture similar to that for the linear model—i.e., general improvement—the indicators are more ambiguous: seven[23] of the estimates show improvement in the trend (i.e., the second derivative), while the three remaining series show improvement in the rate of change to the trend (i.e., the third derivative). However, of the ten estimates, five[24] show worsening in the third derivative: at half of the locations, air quality improves but at a diminishing rate.

SUMMARY AND CONCLUSION

The linear estimates of visibility reduction as an air quality indicator suggest that air quality has been improving. A similar interpretation results when a cubic function is used, with the added benefit of improving the estimate from the standpoint of correcting for autoregressive processes. However, the use of the cubic function introduced an ambiguity into this positive picture: in half of the locations examined, visibility improved at a diminishing rate.

As will be discussed more fully in the next chapter on structural change, the contrast of the cubic with the linear models serves a very useful purpose: comparisons among functional forms allows for the testing of hypotheses about structural change. In general, there are two pieces to the explanation of air quality improvement or deterioration: the technical creation of effluents and the effect of relevant institutions on this "production" process. The crude interpretation is that the linear model demonstrates constant institutional processes, while the cubic function indicates an institutional response that improves (or gets worse) over time.

The analysis so far supports the idea that the processes underlying visibility reduction have dynamic characteristics. However, the incrementalism demonstrated so far is compatible with both the functionalist and utilitarian model. The next chapter's analysis attempts to improve on the simple cubic model. More importantly the next chapter begins to look at how improvements in explanatory power support one political economic model over the other.

NOTES

1. The air quality standards for all primary pollutants are based on the estimated effect on human health.

2. Chapter 6 provides greater detail on these relationships.

3. Barone, et al [1978]; Cass [1979]; Leaderer, Holford and Stolwijk [1979]; Trijonis [1979]; and White and Roberts [1977].

4. Barone, et al [1978]; Lin [1981]; and White and Husar [1976].

5. Cass [1979]; Trijonis [1979]; and White and Roberts [1977].

6. Barone, et al [1978]; Cass, et al [1981]; and White and Roberts [1977].

7. One other directly observable effect of primary pollutants is eye and pulmonary irritation. This does not make for a very tractable dependent variable because there has been no consistent record keeping, the records kept are not of high quality (basically derived from the number of telephone complaints recorded during a day) and the records cover only the period from the mid-1950s.

8. Keith [1980], [1979], and [1964].

9. For all of these data, only readings are counted for days with a relative humidity less than 70 percent. This is the result of deliquescence. Visibility reduction occurs because small particles scatter and absorb light. In the South Coast Air Basin these particles are composed of sulphate, nitrate and elemental carbon derived from pollution, as well as dust. At a relative humidity greater than 70 percent the sulphate and nitrate tend to dissolve or deliquesce so that visibility reduction becomes the result of water vapor rather than the presence of these particle.

10. Keith [1970].

11. U.S. Department of Transportation [1981].

12. Note that in addition to having the "less than seven mile" category, the FAA data differ from the Keith Study in that the FAA Study is based on all observations, while the Keith Study is based on a subset of these—viz., the set of minimum daily observations.

13. Keith [1970].

14. Seven sites are actually listed in the studies. In addition to those listed in the text, downtown Los Angeles and Ontario Airport are included. The former location was included in a separate data set. The latter location, roughly mid-way between downtown and the eastern edged of the SCAB had incomplete and unrecoverable data.

15. Or rather it was upwind until the mill basically shut its doors in 1983.

16. The Norton and March Air Force Base data are generally referred to by the communities in which they are located. Thus Norton AFB becomes San Bernardino and March AFB becomes Riverside.

17. The last year for this series ends before those in the other sites in the Keith Studies because readings ceased at the downtown site when the Los Angeles APCD determined that the data was not worth the cost of recording it.

18. The serial year is the difference between the calendar year of the observation and the first year of the time series.

19. Where the independent variables are the serial year, the square of the serial year and the cube of the serial year.

20. This technically means that it is not possible to distinguish auto-correlation in the independent variable from auto-correlation in the error term. It is the latter condition which defines unacceptable results. See Pindyck and Rubinfeld [1981:152-154, 158-159] and Wonnacott and Wonnacott [1970:137-139].

21. Pindyck and Rubinfeld [1981:117-119]

22. The derivatives of a cubic function

$$f(t) = b_0 + b_1 t + b_2 t^2 + b_3 t^3$$

are

$$\begin{aligned} f' &= b_1 + 2b_2 t + 3b_3 t^2 \\ f'' &= 2b_2 + 6b_3 t \\ f''' &= 6b_3 \end{aligned}$$

23. Three of the variables show unambiguous improvement: downtown Los Angeles average visibility; the Keith SCAQMD accute series for LAX; and the FAA chronic (less than 7 miles) series for LAX. The other four variables—the downtown accute (less than three miles), FAA accute, the Keith SCAQMD Long Beach acute and the Keith SCAQMD San Bernardino series—have second derivatives which show improvement, but the t-statistics is not significant.

24. Three series show unambiguous worsening—the downtown Los Angeles average, the Keith SCAQMD acute (less than 3 miles) and the FAA chronic (less than 7 miles) series. The two other series—the downtown Los Angeles acute and the FAA acute series—show worsening in the third derivative, but the t-statistic is not significant.

REFERENCES CITED

Barone, J.B., et al. 1978. A multivariate statistical analysis of visibility degradation at four California cities. *Atmospheric environments*. 12 (1978), 2213-2221.

Cass, Glen, et al. 1981. Wintertime carbonaceous aerosols in Los Angeles: an exploration of thhe role of elemental carbon. *American Chemical Society symposium series 167*.

Cass, Glen. 1979. On the relationship between sulfate air quality and visibility with examples in Los Angeles. *Atmospheric environments*. 13 (1979), 1069-1084.

Douville, Judith. 1981. Indexing and abstracting services in the air pollution field. *Journal of the Air Pollution Control Association*. 31:4 (April, 1981), 361-364.

Keith, Ralph. 1980. A climatological-air quality profile: California South Coast Air Basin. *South Coast Air Quality Management District*. (November, 1980).

Keith, Ralph. 1979. Low visibility trends in the South Coast Air Basin (1950-1977). *South Coast Air Quality Management District*. (January, 1979).

Keith, Ralph. 1970. Downtown Los Angeles noon visibility trends, 1933-1969. *Los Angeles Air Pollution Control District, Report No. 65*. (December 15, 1970).

Keith, Ralph. 1964. A study of low visibility trends in the Los Angeles Basin, 1950-1961. *Los Angeles Air Pollution Control District, Report No. 53*. (January, 1964).

Leaderer, Brian, Holford, Theodore and Stolwijk, Jan. 1979. Relationship between sulfate aerosol and visibility. *Journal of the Air Pollution Control Association*. 29:2 (January, 1979), 154-157.

Lin, Gong-Yuh. 1981. Simple markov chain model of smog probability in the South Coast Air Basin of California. *Professional geographer*. 33:2 (1981), 228-236.

Pindyck, Robert and Rubinfeld, Daniel. 1981. *Econometric models and economic forecasts*. New York: McGraw-Hill.

Tiao, G.C. , Phadle, M.S. and Box, G.E.P.. 1976. Some empirical models for the Los Angeles photochemical smog data. *Journal of the Air Pollution Control Association*. 26:5 (May, 1976), 485-490.

Trijonis, John. 1979. Visibility in the Southwest--an exploration of the historial data base. *Atmospheric environments*. 13 (1979), 833-843.

U.S. Department of Transportation, Federal Aviation Administration. 1981. *Wind-ceiling-visibility data at selected airports*. (June, 1981).

White, Warren H. and Husar, Rudolf B. 1976. A lagrangian model of the Los Angeles smog aerosol. *Journal of the Air Pollution Control Association*. 26:1 (January, 1976), 32-35.

White, Warren H. and Roberts, P.T. 1977. On the nature and origins of visibility-reducing aerosols in the Los Angeles Air Basin. *Atmospheric environments*. 11 (1977), 803-812.

Wonnacott, Ronald and Wonnacott, Thomas. 1970. *Econometrics*. Toronto: John Wiley and Sons.

CHAPTER 5

Structural Change

Because of the nature of the air pollution problem, the phrase "the structural causes of smog" and along with it the phrase "structural change in air quality" can each mean two different things. On the one hand, air pollution can change for technical reasons almost entirely unrelated to actions attributable to the institutions responsible for air pollution control. For example, the oil embargo of the early 1970s caused dramatic reductions in the amount of driving done by people in Southern California. The data might spuriously associate a structural change in air pollution control with a shift in the trend in visibility reduction brought about by the embargo. In controlling for mobile source activity, for example, this effect can be removed from the regression analysis.

THE FUNCTIONAL FORM OF THE ESTIMATOR

The basic functionalist model used for hypothesizing about the structural determinants of visibility reduction is expressed in the following notation and graphical representation. The fundamental concept is that the purely technical causes of visibility reduction have developed in a statistically neutral way because smog is not a relevant consideration when the techniques whose application cause air pollution are selected and used.[1] What affects change is not technical decisionmaking per se, but the effect of institutions on those decisions. These relationships are presented in functional notation below.

$$v_i = \text{visibility reduction in period } i \qquad (5\text{-}1)$$
$$= f(r_i; s_i)$$

where

r_i =   effect of institutions on control of air pollution source activity in period i

s_i =   source activity causing visibility reduction in period i

$f(s_i)$ =   visibility reduction due to technical effects alone

$f(r_i; s_i)$ =   visibility reduction due to technical effects modified by regulatory action

Figure 5-1 below borrows from Figure 2-8 in Chapter 2. The solid line represents the actual air quality index. Prior to the initiation of regulatory activity, the only effect was due to source activity—the institutional effect is negligible. Air quality with and without an institutional variable will be the same—$f(s_i) = f(r_i; s_i)$. After the initiation of regulation, air quality improves—equal to $f(r_i; s_i)$. Counterfactually, if regulation had not occurred the trend prevailing before regulation would have continued—equal to $f(r_i; s_i)$.

It is useful at this point to return to the interpretation of the linear and cubic models introduced in the last chapter. The meaning of the two functional forms is related directly to the distinction between structural change in technical versus institutional causes of visibility reduction.

The results of a linear model are straightforward: the trend estimated is the combined result of the effect of technical change and changes in the effectiveness of air pollution control institutions.

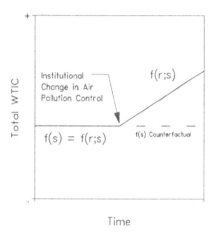

Figure 5-1

Air quality trends and structural change showing technical and institutional factors

Figure 5-1 graphically represents this result: structural change in the linear model results in changes to the slope of the line. Underlying this kind of estimate is the idea that the effectiveness of the institution is constant with respect to time. That is, the institutions become neither relatively better nor worse at their mission over time.

The results of the cubic regression can also be hypothesized to have a technical and institutional component. The additional feature of this type of model is that it can accommodate institutional effectiveness that itself changes over time. The effect of pure technics growing over time can also be represented in this model.

If the technical relationship between source activity and visibility reduction is linear, then the estimator for this relationship is given by

$$v_i = \beta_0 + b_1 s_i \tag{5-2}$$

The effect of regulatory institutions on visibility reduction can be represented in one of two ways: as an additive adjustment to the technical relationship; or as a weight on the technical relationship. Heuristically, either relationship represents the idea that institutional activity directly adjusts the technical relationship—for example, requiring the implementation of techniques that reduce the impact of source activity on visibility reduction. The additive relationship can be represented as

$$v_i = \beta_0 + (b_1 + r)s_i$$
$$= \beta_0 + b_1 s_i + r s_i \qquad (5\text{-}3)$$

The multiplicative relationship can be represented as

$$v_i = \beta_0 + b_1 r s_i \qquad (5\text{-}4)$$

The rate of change in air quality with respect to source activity will therefore be the first derivative of either equation (5-3)—i.e., the coefficient $(b_1 + r)$—or equation (5-4)—i.e., the coefficient $(b_1 r)$. The interpretation of these is that the rate of change is constant for a given technical regime and institutional structure. Structural change results in a change of the slope to a new constant.

On this interpretation, visibility reduction changes solely as a function of source activity. This translates easily into the linear model introduced in the previous chapter: if source activity has a rate of change over time, so will visibility reduction. The interpretation of the results in the previous chapter (i.e., the general improvement in visibility reduction) in the face of growing source activity is that regulatory institutions more than offset the technical relationship.

However, the technical and institutional relationships may be affected by the passage of time. It seems reasonable to suppose that over time pollution sources will attempt to economize on the fuel burned and otherwise make more efficient use of materials that are transformed in the production process into commodities and effluents. It also seems reasonable to hypothesize that a kind of institutional learning takes place: enforcement personnel find ways of being more effective with specific sources; while activists and polluters learn how to be more effective in the political process.[2] This situation can be represented by

$$r = k + mt_i \tag{5-5}$$

where t_i is the serial year.

This equation represents the idea of incrementalism in technical and institutional development. If equation (5-4)—the multiplicative relationship—is the correct specification, then combining and reducing equations (5-4) and (5-5) gives a slope or rate of change to (5-4) that is linear and specified by equation (5-6) below.

$$b_1 r = b_1 k + b_1 m t_i \tag{5-6}$$

If equation (5-3)—the additive relationship—is the correct specification, then the first derivative, assuming (5-4) and (5-5) to be true, will be the linear function given in equation (5-7) below.

$$b_1 + r = b_1 + k + m t_i \tag{5-7}$$

The additive relationship and the multiplicative relationship will reduce to a linear function that expresses the slope of the dependent variable with respect to time. The estimator is given by equation (5-8) below.

$$v_i = \beta_0 + \beta_1 s_i + \beta_2 s_i t_i \tag{5-8}$$

For the additive relationship, $\beta_1 = b_1 + k$ and $\beta_2 = m$. For the multiplicative relationship, $\beta_1 = b_1 k$ and $\beta_2 = b_1 m$.

The immediate and obvious problem with this functional form is the problem of collinearity[3]: an independent variable that is a linear function of another independent variable. The problem this creates is that the estimators have no independent meaning since the meaning of the coefficient associated with a regressor is its effect on the dependent variable with all other variables held constant.

In this situation there are two saving graces to this problem. First, the functional form given is an attempt to disaggregate what is obviously a unified process. No attempt is made to independently evaluate the coefficient for source activity in the absence of the institutional effect suggested by equation (5-8). Second, as the model is developed in this chapter the institutional variable represented by $s_i t_i$

in equation (5-8) is subjected to partitioning into several pieces thus creating discontinuities with the linear relationship to source activity simpliciter.

THE ANALYSIS OF STRUCTURAL CHANGE

The analysis of time series is frequently concerned not only with trends but also with changes in trends. In particular, what generally interests economists is not the behavior of a time series itself but the relationship between the underlying process and the observed data. When structural change in the underlying process occurs, the analyst expects and wants to test for this change in the observed data. A classic kind of application is the use of dummy variables to separate time series of macroeconomic activity that span World War II into pre-war and post-war trends.[4]

The limitation on the use of dummy variables is that their application does not allow for the estimation of structural change that maintains continuity over time. For example, the introduction of a new technology may have a specific date when it first appears but requires many years for its ubiquitous introduction. In order to address this limitation, economists and statisticians introduced the use of spline functions to time series modelling. The use of spline functions in economic analysis was first introduced and developed by Dale Poirier.[5] Poirier gives the following definition for a spline function:

> A polynomial spline of degree n is a piecewise polynomial function made up of polynomials of degree at most n such that the spline and its derivatives up to and including the $(n - 1)^{th}$ are continuous.[6]

The application as developed by Poirier was simplified by Buse and Lim[7] in order to make estimation more tractable. The function most commonly used in these analyses is the cubic or third degree polynomial.[8] This type of function has some useful properties for the analysis of time series when structural change is a consideration.[9] Namely, the first and second derivatives of a cubic polynomial correspond to, respectively, the rate of change in the independent variable and the rate at which this rate of change itself changes.

The tests for structural change begin with the specification of a date or point in the dependent variable series at which structural change is hypothesized to have occurred. These points are referred to in the literature as "knots." Each knot and the first and last data point demarcate a set of segments or pieces of the dependent variable, such that for a series with k knots there will be $(k + 1)$ pieces. Spline functions make it possible to create a model with estimators for each piece with restrictions on these estimators so that there is continuity of the estimate at each of the knots. This is done by setting restrictions on the regression so that the estimates for the piece and the first through the $(n - 1)^{th}$ derivatives for the piece on the other side of the knot, are equal at each knot.

For a time series that covers the years 1933 to 1979, hypotheses about the behavior of the series before and after World War II can be made. This would mean establishing a knot at 1945, with two pieces—1933 to 1944 and 1945 to 1979. Continuity is established by requiring that the estimate along with the $(n - 1)^{th}$ derivatives be equal when the parameters for the first and second piece are evaluated at the knot. In this case, the dependent variable along with the first through the $(n - 1)^{th}$ derivatives of the regression equation for the first piece (1933 to 1944) evaluated at the knot (i.e., at 1945) are made equal to the estimate of the dependent variable and first $(n - 1)$ derivatives of the regression equation for the second piece (1945 to 1979) evaluated at the knot (i.e., at 1945).

A cubic estimator is defined as

$$y = f(x)$$
$$= b_0 + b_1 x + b_2 x^2 + b_3 x^3 \tag{5-9}$$

The spline function for each piece is distinguished so that there is a first, 1933-to-1944 piece and a second, 1945-to-1979 piece. That is,

$$y = f(x_{1933-44}) + g(x_{1945-79}) \tag{5-10}$$

The restrictions on this equation that satisfy the continuity requirements are given by the following conditions. First, the estimates of the dependent variables must be equal at the knot.

$$f(x_{1945}) = g(x_{1945}) \tag{5-11}$$

which for the cubic function translates into

$$b1_0 + b1_2 x_{1945} + b1_1 x_{1945}^2 + b1_3 x_{1945}^3$$
$$= b2_0 + b2_1 x_{1945} + b2_2 x_{1945}^2 + b2_3 x_{1945}^3 \tag{5-12}$$

Second, the first derivatives of the regression equations for each piece must be equal at the knot.

$$f'(x_{1945}) = g'(x_{1945}) \tag{5-13}$$

which for the cubic function translates into

$$b1_1 + 2b1_2 x_{1945} + 3b1_3 x_{1945}^2$$
$$= b2_1 + 2b2_2 x_{1945} + 3b2_3 x_{1945}^2 \tag{5-14}$$

Third, the second derivatives of the regression equations for each piece must be equal at the knot.

$$f''(x_{1945}) = g''(x_{1945}) \tag{5-15}$$

which for the cubic function translates into

$$2b1_2 + 6b1_3 x_{1945} = 2b2_2 + 6b2_3 x_{1945} \tag{5-16}$$

Hypothesis testing can then proceed by comparing the estimates of the restricted versus the unrestricted estimate of the dependent variable using a standard F-test. The primary test performed is the meaningfulness of partitioning the time series into $k + 1$ pieces and the meaningfulness of the placement of the k knots. Using this restricted least squares method is cumbersome but tractable. However, a more transparent and more malleable method has been developed.

Suits, Mason and Chan[10] developed a standard ordinary least squares regression procedure that not only is comparable to the restricted least squares method in estimating structural change, but also is much more amenable to model building and testing. The method can work on any degree polynomial function, but for the purpose of model building (and for ease of exposition) a linear function will be used. Continuing the example above, let the time series extend from 1933 to 1979 with a knot at 1945. Dummy variables are introduced, so that

$$d_i \begin{cases} = 1 \; for \; piece \; i \\ = 0 \; for \; all \; other \; pieces \end{cases} \qquad (5\text{-}17)$$

The regression equation is expressed as

$$y_i = \{b1_0 + b1_1(x_i - x_{1933})\}d_1 + \{b2_0 + b2_1(x_i - x_{1945})\}d_2 \qquad (5\text{-}18)$$

In the case of linear spline functions, the continuity requirement is satisfied by requiring the intercepts to be equal at the knot. This means that

$$b1_0 + b1_1(x_{1945} - x_{1933}) = b2_0 + b2_1(x_{1945} - x_{1945}) \qquad (5\text{-}19)$$

This in turn reduces to

$$b2_0 = b1_0 + b1_1(x_{1945} - x_{1933}) \qquad (5\text{-}20)$$

With the substitution of equation (5-20) into equation (19), the regression equation can be simplified to

$$y_i = \{b1_0 + b1_1(x_i - x_{1933})\}(d_1 + d_2) + \{(b2_1 + b1_1)(x_i - x_{1945})\}d_2 \qquad (5\text{-}21)$$

This in turn will reduce to a regression equation with three parameters.

$$y_i = b1_0 + b1_1(x_i - x_{1933}) + B2_1(x_i - x_{1945})d_2 \qquad (5\text{-}22)$$

Where

$$B2_1 = b2_1 + b1_1 \qquad (5\text{-}23)$$

These results can be generalized to models with more than one knot and with higher degree polynomials. To simplify the notation, the knots will be denoted by their position in the sequence of the time series (i.e., knot 1, knot 2, etc., instead of "the knot at 1945") and the independent variable will be subscripted to denote the difference between the value of the variable and the subscripted value at the knot. Thus x_1 will denote the difference between the independent variable and the value of that variable at the first knot (e.g., in the example above this would be $x_i - x_{1945}$). If a model is to be tested which specifies two knots instead of one, then the regression equation would look like

$$y = bl_0 + bl_1x_1 + B2_1x_2(d_2 + d_3) + B3_1x_3d_3 \qquad (5\text{-}24)$$

In general,

$$Bi_1 = bi_1 + \sum_{k=1}^{i-1} b(k)_1 \qquad (5\text{-}25)$$

To fully generalize this model to the case where the regression equation is an n-degree polynomial and the model is testing the meaningfulness of k knots in the time series, the regression equation becomes

$$y = \sum_{h=0}^{n} bl_h x_1^h + \sum_{i=2}^{k} Bi_n x_i^n \sum_{j=i}^{k} d_j \qquad (5\text{-}26)$$

With this form, tests on the meaningfulness of the location of knots are simply a test of the hypothesis that each, all or some combination of the parameters Bp_n are statistically significant. Moreover, this formulation makes it easy to construct multiple regression models with independent variables having either different functional forms (i.e., polynomials of different degrees) or independent variables having knots located at different places along the time series or both. To take the simplest case, an additional variable could be added to the general equation (5-26), (5-27). Let this be a variable z having g total knots and having the functional form of a polynomial of degree r. The dummy variables associated with each variable/knot location are designated appropriately. Then the 2-variable model will be

$$y = \sum_{h=0}^{n} b1_h x_1^h + \sum_{i=2}^{k} Bi_n x_i^n \sum_{j=i}^{k} d_k + \sum_{r=1}^{p} c1_r z_1^r + \sum_{s=2}^{l} Cs_p z_s^p \sum_{t=s}^{l} d_t \qquad (5\text{-}27)$$

STRUCTURAL CHANGE IN VISIBILITY REDUCTION

In this section a simple piecewise regression model is evaluated for all locations. This simple piecewise model is a development of the regression equations used in the previous chapter. A two-piece and a three-piece model are compared to the one-piece, ordinary least squares results using the cubic functional form. The evaluation of results is in terms of the ability of piecewise models to improve on the one-piece model. The results are given in Appendix E.

The meaning behind why knots were place where they were is briefly summarized in Table 5-I below. The location of the knots represents structural change. What the location of these knots tests is the idea that the "market" for air quality experiences a shift in the supply or demand function for clean air—i.e., when the rules of the game changed. Because of the conception of the superstructure as a unified whole, the alternative functionalist model would tend to view the history of the structural determinants of air quality as relatively seamless.

Local, stationary source regulation became a political issue during World War II with the first regulatory efforts beginning in 1946. The creation of the Los Angeles Air Pollution Control District occurred in 1948. By the late-1950s all four of the counties studied here had created Air Pollution Control Districts. In the mid-1950s the Los Angeles APCD had undergone a restructuring of the agency. Also in the mid-1950s the nature of the physical processes involved in the production of air pollution had been clearly identified along with the role of the automobile. No basic structural change occurs in the operation of the APCDs until the creation of the South Coast Air Quality Management

Table 5-I

Years of Significant Structural Change

Year	Change
1944	Air pollution gets on the political agenda in Los Angeles
1946	First regulatory efforts by Los Angeles city and county
1948	Los Angeles County Air Pollution Control District formed
1956	All four counties within the South Coast Air Basin have formed Air Pollution Control Districts
	Discovery and acceptance of photochemical nature of smog, including implications for mobile and stationary sources
1960	Southern California freeway begins rapid expansion
	California Motor Vehicle Control Board is created, formally separating mobile (state) from stationary (local) source control
1964	Citizen activists become major critics of the Los Angeles Air Pollution Control District
1968	California Air Resources Board formed, establishing state requirements for mobile and pollution source control
	The environmental movement becomes an significant social force
1970	Clean Air Act passed, establishing Federal pre-eminence in stationary and mobile source control
1974	Restructuring Southern California air pollution control becomes a major issue on the political agenda at the local and state level
	Southern California freeway system ends its period rapid expansion
1976	South Coast Air Quality Management District formed, combining air pollution agencies in four counties
1977	Federal Clean Air Act significantly amended, including economic tools such as bubble policies and pollution offsets

District in 1976 and the political actions that immediately preceded its creation. As a consequence 1948, 1956 and 1976 are important knots from the standpoint of local institutional development—i.e., as shifts in the supply function for air quality, especially air quality effects resulting from stationary sources.

From the demand function side 1944 is an important location for a knot because it effectively marks the arrival of air pollution on the political agenda. 1974 is also an important knot location because of the focused effort to restructure air quality control in the South Coast Air Basin—i.e., as shifts in the demand function for air quality. The effect on air quality trends of these knots should be positive.

State and Federal intervention in air pollution control, at least from an institutional as opposed to an advisory role, appears with the creation of the Air Resources Board in California in 1968 and with the enactment of the Clean Air Act of 1970 and its subsequent amendment in 1977. The major impact of the ARB prior to the Clean Air Act is on mobile source activity. After the Clean Air Act the ARB became responsible for managing the implementation of mobile source control and for overseeing the implementation by local APCDs of stationary source controls. A knot is therefore located at 1968 to represent the beginning of mobile source control—i.e., a shift in the supply function.

Local planning agencies have two turning points. Of primary interest is the commitment in the mid-1950s to the freeway system which appeared by the late-1950s and early-1960s as a rapid increase in the miles of freeway constructed. This transportation development completed its rapid growth phase by the late-1960s and early-1970s. The growth in the transportation system is as much indicative of the general dispersal of economic activity throughout the South Coast Air Basin as it is indicative of the expansion of the opportunity to promote mobile source activity. A knot at 1960 and at 1974 capture the beginning and ending points of this growth—i.e., a shift in the supply function for air quality. The effect of this potential shift should be negative.

Citizen activism is best demarcated by the rise in the early 1960s of an identifiable environmental movement. In terms of local air pollution politics there was a shift in the mid-1960s by activists from a role that was basically supportive of the APCDs (responsible for putatively controlled stationary sources) to an adversarial role with respect to local regulators. A knot is therefore located in 1964 as a shift in the demand function, with the expected effect of improving the impact of air quality institutions.

PIECEWISE ANALYSIS OF VISIBILITY TRENDS

In addition to the straightforward linear and cubic functions introduced in the last chapter, two additional functions are evaluated here: a two- and three-piece regression equation for the cubic functional form. In the following specifications, these conventions will be used

$$d_2 \begin{cases} = 1 \text{ } \textit{for piece } 2 \\ = 0 \text{ } \textit{for all other pieces} \end{cases}$$

$$d_3 \begin{cases} = 1 \text{ } \textit{for piece } 3 \\ = 0 \text{ } \textit{for all other pieces} \end{cases}$$

$t1$ = serial year
    = calendar year - first year of series

$t2$ = serial year from knot separating first from second piece
    = calendar year - year defining first knot

$t3$ = serial year from knot separating second from third piece
    = calendar year - year defining second knot

The two-piece cubic model is

$$v_i = b1_0 + b1_1 t1 + b1_2 t1^2 + b1_3 t1^3 + B2_3 t2^3 d_2 \tag{5-28}$$

The three-piece cubic model is

$$v_i = b1_0 + b1_1 t1 + b1_2 t1^2 + b1_3 t1^3 + B2_3 t2^3 (d_2 + d_3) + B3_3 t3^3 d_3 \tag{5-29}$$

The results of the best piecewise regressions using a cubic model compared to the one-piece cubic models are given in Table 5-II below. Each of the models list's had statistically significant results (refer to Chapter 4). The complete results are shown Appendix E. Of the ten locations, five show improvements in the estimates when a piecewise model is applied. Moreover, there is something of a pattern that

Table 5-II

Comparison of Piecewise Cubic Function Showing Statistically Significant
Improvement over One-Piece Cubic Function

Location Dependent Variable	1st Knot	2nd Knot	Trends	
			1st Derivative	2nd Derivative
Downtown LA				
<7 Miles	1964	1974	Improve	Worsen (1933-64)
				Improve (1964-74)
				Worsen (1974-79)
Average Minimum	1944	1956	Worsen	Improve (1933-44)
				Worsen (1944-56)
				Improve (1956-79)
Los Angeles International Airport				
< 3 Miles (Keith)	1960	1968	Improve	Worsen (1950-60)
				Improve (1960-68)
				Worsen (1968-82)
Burbank < 3 Miles	1960	1968	Improve	Worsen (1950-60)
				Improve (1960-68)
				Worsen (1968-82)

develops: four of the seven show improvements with knots at 1974; two others show improvements with a three-piece model with knots at 1960 and 1968. The 1974 knots generally implicate a worsening due to mobile source activity as a result of the termination of the freeway system. The 1960/1968 regressions implicate the transportation system as well: the third derivative (rate of change in the trend) shows improvement in the inter-knot period when growth in the system began and transportation corridors opened up, terminated by worsening of the rate of change in the trend when the system's growth ceased.

SUMMARY AND CONCLUSION

The results in this chapter darken the picture painted in the last chapter. The number of estimates showing improvement in the second derivative (what is referred to here as the trend) shrank from nine to seven; the number of estimates showing improvement in the third derivative (the rate of change in the trend) diminished from six to four.

Two important observations result from this comparison: no powerful pattern emerges; and, the patterns that do emerge seem to be more closely related to events outside the control of the institutions responsible for air quality control. Although the 1944/1956 knots for the average daily minimum time series in downtown Los Angeles correspond to a shift in the demand function for air quality, the result is isolated.

The important questions to be answered in the next chapter have to do with the explanation of what happened. With the introduction of a causal model to estimate trends, it will turn out that many of the apparent structural changes in the trends are explicable in terms of source activity alone.

NOTES

1. Which is to say that air pollution is an unintended effect of source activity—i.e., an externality.

2. It is certainly true that the people currently involved with air pollution control are much more sophisticated both technically and institutionally than their counterparts were forty years ago.

3. Pindyck and Rubinfeld [1981:87-88]; Wonnacott and Wonnacott [1970:59-61].

4. Wonnacott and Wonnacott [1970 : 68-72].

5. Poirier [1976] and [1973].

6. Poirier [1976 : 2]. The introductory chapter of Poirier's book (from which the quote is taken) gives a history of the function and its application.

7. Buse and Lim [1977].

8. That is, a function of the form $y = a + bx + cx^2 + dx^3$.

9. However, the polynomial function tends not to be very useful for forecasting.

10. Chan, Mason and Suits [1978].

REFERENCES

Bishop, Robert V. 1981. The use and misuse of summary statistics in regression analysis. *Agricultural economics research*. 33:1 (January, 1981), 13-18.

Buse, A. and Lim, L. 1977. Cubic splines as a special case of restricted least squares. *Journal of the American Statistical Association*. 72:357 (1977), 64-68.

Chan, Louis, Mason, Andrew and Suits, Daniel. 1978. Spline functions fitted by standard regression methods. *Review of economics and statistics*. 60 (February, 1978), 132-139.

Pindyck, Robert and Rubinfeld, Daniel. 1981. *Econometric models and economic forecasts*. New York: McGraw-Hill.

Poirier, Dale J. 1976. *The econometrics of structural change*. New York: North-Holland.

Poirier, Dale J. 1973. Piecewise regression using splines. *Journal of the American Statistical Association*. 68:343 (September, 1973), 515-521.

Wonnacott, Ronald and Wonnacott, Thomas. 1970. *Econometrics*. Toronto: John Wiley and Sons.

CHAPTER 6

Air Quality And Institutional Change

In this chapter the visibility reduction data analyzed in the last two chapters is compared to underlying causal relationships. The discussion is concerned primarily with the relationship between visibility reduction, the production of primary pollutants[1] and the institutional changes that have occurred in Southern California over the last fifty years.

The data used in the analysis are found in Appendix F. The interpretation of the results given at the end of the chapter supports the functionalist theory. The results support the theory by showing that, when the model is controlled for basic source activity, no significant improvement in explanatory power is realized when the data are segmented to account for institutional change.

As discussed previously, the contrast between the functionalist and utilitarian theories depends on what counts as a significant change in the institutional rules of the game. Institutional change occurs in the utilitarian model when there is a significant change in the conditions in which the relevant trade-offs take place—i.e., when there is a change in the conditions of supply or demand for improved air quality. The market equivalent would be a shift in the supply or demand function. In the functionalist theory, it is not the conditions for the "market" for air quality which are subject to change but the entire superstructure of which such a "market" is a part. Given stability in that superstructure, the conditions for the control of air quality—and hence air quality itself as an outcome—will likewise remain stable.

153

THE CAUSES OF VISIBILITY REDUCTION

Visibility reduction is the result of combustion processes used by air pollution sources. These sources fall technically and institutionally into two categories: mobile and stationary. At its simplest level, regulatory activity is focused on the combustion processes of each of these kinds of sources. Mobile and stationary sources burn fuels, which in turn produce effluents. The regulated effluents are monitored directly or are indirectly monitored through the activity itself. Visibility is not regulated, but it does have a systematic relationship with effluents that are regulated.

Table 6-I
Relationship of primary pollutants to visibility reducing effluents

Primary Pollutant	Visibility Reducing Effluent or Photochemical Product
Sulphur dioxide	Sulphate
Nitrogen oxide Nitrogen dioxide	Nitrate
Reactive hydrocarbons Carbon monoxide	Elemental carbon

There are two circumstances affecting primary pollutants and visibility reducing effluents. On the one hand, there is the purely technical relationship of the fuel burned and the cumbustion technology employed (e.g., internal combustion engines with and without catalytic converters). On the other hand, there is the decision-making process regarding the selection and relative intensity of use of fuels and technologies.

Visibility reducing effluents of combustion are a result of aerosol chemistry—light scattering (and light absorption) by material suspended in the air (referred to as total suspended particulates or TSP). The primary meteorological condition affecting visibility reduction is relative humidity. The effluents that most affect visibility reduction are sulphate, nitrate and elemental carbon.

Sulphate becomes an effluent from combustion processes as a result of the sulphur content of fuels burned. All fossil fuels have some elemental sulphur in them: sulphur combines with atmospheric oxygen during combustion to form sulphur dioxide; in the atmosphere some of this sulphur dioxide is transformed into sulphate.[2] The ambient atmospheric concentration of sulphur dioxide is a primary pollution standard. In general, sulphurous effluents are associated with stationary sources.

Nitrate becomes an effluent from combustion processes as a result of the heat produced in the burning of fuels. During combustion the heat released combines atmospheric nitrogen and atmospheric oxygen to form nitrogen dioxide and nitrogen oxide. The most important atmospheric reaction that these nitrogen oxides participate in is the formation of photochemical oxidant. In addition, nitrogen oxides are transformed in the atmosphere into nitrate.[3] The ambient atmospheric concentration of nitrogen oxides is a primary pollutant standard. In general nitrogen oxides are associated with mobile sources, although less exclusively than the relationship of sulphur to the burning of fossil fuels by stationary sources.

Elemental carbon becomes an effluent from combustion processes as a result of inefficient combustion. Completely efficient combustion of a "pure" fossil fuel (i.e., a fuel composed of organic compounds consisting of carbon and hydrogen only) would result in the production of heat, carbon dioxide and water vapor. Inefficient combustion results in the release of elemental carbon particles and the primary pollutants carbon monoxide and the complex hydrocarbons that contribute to the formation of photochemical oxidants.[4] Elemental carbon is associated primarily with mobile sources because of the inherent inefficiencies in fuel combustion over the driving cycle (i.e., start-up, acceleration, deceleration, and cruise); elemental carbon is especially associated with diesel engines.

The effect of combustion technologies results from two selection processes: the decision of the technology itself, and the when and where to use the technology. The selection of a combustion technology consists of two decisions: the selection of a combustion technique based on the requirements for heat generation and the economics of the technology selected; and the selection of the fuel to be used in the combustion process based on the fuel requirements for the process and the economics of the fuel selected. The second decision is how the technology is actually used in practice as one among a mix of possible sources of heat or energy. The actual practice has two aspects: the timing of the combustion process—i.e., when a particular technology is used during the day or during the year; and the amount or extent to which a technology is used in relation to other available technologies.

The best example of these technology selection processes is the mode of production for a large electric generating company such as Southern California Edison. Such a company will have a mix of sources it will use in generating electricity: wind turbines, turbines powered by fossil fuel or natural gas, hydroelectric dams, fluidized bed reactor co-generation and nuclear power plants. Each type of electricity generating technique has its own unique generating capabilities, cost structure, fuel requirements and optimal operating characteristics.

Pollution source activity is the focal point of the regulatory effort. Historically, regulation has focused on the critical points in the combustion selection process undertaken by a polluter. However, in the case of visibility reduction, the regulatory effort has had its effect indirectly: sulphur emissions have been regulated to reduce sulphur dioxide; nitrogen oxide emissions have been regulated primarily to control the emissions that contribute to the formation of photochemical oxidant and secondarily to reduce nitrogen oxide effluents; the emissions of organic compounds have been regulated to control the hydrocarbon effluents that contribute to the formation of photochemical oxidant and the emissions of carbon monoxide.

The actual methods used for affecting the emissions of primary pollutants have focused on the two combustion technology selection process. The control of the actual heat producing combustion technology, including both process and fuel selection, has been the prevailing approach to controlling effluents. This has been used to affect sulphur effluents, for example, by permitting only the use of fuels with a low sulphur content by stationary sources. For mobile sources the regulation of fuel selection has not affected carbon-based effluents, but has been aimed at the emissions of lead. The control of the timing of fuel use and the mix of combustion processes used has been a lesser used method. Timing of combustion, from a regulatory point of view, is determined primarily by meteorological conditions. For example, the first requlations requiring the substitution of low sulphur for high sulphur fuels were implemented only for the severe smog season (roughly from May through September). The final piece of the regulatory picture is unrelated to both combustion and source activity. Since visibility reduction (and the effect of primary pollutants) is heavily affected by meteorological conditions, part of the timing of combustion is determined by meteorological conditions per se. In particular, this means the formation of the inversion layer that traps effluents in the Los Angeles airshed to be "cooked" by solar energy.

REGRESSION ANALYSIS OF DOWNTOWN LOS ANGELES

This section evaluates estimates for the three long term (1933-1979) downtown Los Angeles series based on the relationships discussed in the previous chapter. However, this model is incomplete because it lacks any adjustment for meteorology and does not control for mobile source activity. Thus the conclusions drawn from this analysis can be indicative only—the results will require confirmation by the complete model developed in the next section. Six models are evaluated: a one-, two- and three-piece causal model and symmetrically a one-, two- and three-piece institutional model. The independent variable used in these models—i.e., the measure of source activity—is manufacturing employment in the Los Angeles Standard Metropolitan Statistical Area from 1935 to 1979. The data are given in Appendix F. In the specification of the model, the following conventions will be used:

$d_2 \begin{cases} = 1 \ \textit{for piece 2} \\ = 0 \ \textit{for all other pieces} \end{cases}$

$d_3 \begin{cases} = 1 \ \textit{for piece 3} \\ = 0 \ \textit{for all other pieces} \end{cases}$

$t \quad = \quad$ serial year

$E \quad = \quad$ manufacturing employement

$E(i)$ =   manufacturing for piece i (from knot i-1 to knot i)

   = $E - E_{knot\ i-1}$

R =   institutional variable

   = Et

$R(i)$ =   institutional variable for piece i (from knot i-1 to knot i)

   = $R - R_{knot\ i-1}$

Bi_j =   coefficient for i^{th} piece of the jth independent variable, where j takes values E (manufacturing employment) or R (institutional variable)

   = $bi_j + \sum\limits_{k=1}^{i-1} b(k)_j$

The one piece causal model is

$$v = b1_0 + b1_E E(1) \tag{6-1}$$

The two-piece causal model is

$$v = b1_0 + b1_E E(1) + B2_E E(2)d_2 \tag{6-2}$$

The three-piece causal model is

$$v = b1_0 + b1_E E(1) + B2_E E(2)d_2 + B3_E E(3)d_3 \tag{6-3}$$

The one piece institutional model is

$$v = b1_0 + b1_E E(1) + b1_R R(1) \tag{6-4}$$

The two-piece institutional model is

$$v = b1_0 + b1_E E(1) + b1_R R(1) + B2_R R(2)d_2 \tag{6-5}$$

The three-piece institutional model is

$$v = b1_0 + b1_E E(1) + b1_R R(1) + B2_R R(2)d_2 + B3_R R(3)d_3 \quad (6\text{-}6)$$

A summary of the results from these regressions is contained in Table 6-II and Table 6-III below. A complete set of results is contained in Appendix G.

Table 6-II

Comparison of summary statistics for causal and instituional models
downtown Los Angeles, 1935-79

Dependent Variable	Addition of Institutional Variable Improves			Effect of Each Variable on Trend		
				Manufacturing		
	R^2	F Value	Durban-Watson	Without Institutional Variable	With Institutional Variable	Institutional Variable
Avg Min	No	Yes	Yes	No Change	Worsen	Improve
< 3 Miles	No	Yes	Yes	Improve	Worsen	Improve
< 7 Miles	No	Yes	Yes	No Change	Worsen	Improve

Table 6-II appears to show that the simple causal model cannot be improved on by the institutional model in explaining the trend in visibility: although the institutional model improved on the causal model in the significance of the regression (*F*-test) and in compensating for autoregression (Durbin-Watson), it provides a *less* powerful result in explaining variation in the independent variable (adjusted R^2). Despite this poor performance, the institutional model is clearly superior to the causal model because it shows the correct relationship between source activity and visibility: as manufacturing employment increases, visibility worsens; the value of the coefficient for the institutional variable indicates a positive effect on visibility.

Table 6-III shows the results from the piecewise regression of the institutional model. The complete results are given in Appendix G. In general these results tend to reinforce the results from the simple trend analysis given in the previous chapter: 1974 emerges as a year in which structural change is evident, and that the result of the structural change was negative for the severe (less than three miles) and chronic (less than seven miles) episodes; 1944 emerges again as an important year

Table 6-III

Effect of piecewise model on institutional model

Dependent Variable	Year of Knot		Effect of Each Variable on Trend	
	1st	2nd	Manufacturing	Institutional
< 3 Miles	1968	1974	No Change	Worsen
				Improve
				Worsen
< 7 Miles	1968	1974	Worsen	Improve
				Improve
				Worsen
Average Min	1944	1968	Worsen	Worsen
				Improve
				Improve

for the general air quality indicator (average minimum) indicating improvement in air quality. However, complete confirmation of these results must come from the fully specified model developed in the next section.

The relationships modelled in the previous section are indicative of the desired specification for a complete model. However, the specification of this simple causal model are incomplete. By developing the relationships explicated at the beginning of this chapter, a fully specified function can be derived. In functional notation, this function can be specified in the following way:

$$v_i = f(r_i, s_i; l_i, m_i; w_i) \qquad (6\text{-}7)$$

Where

v_i = visibility reduction in period i

r_i = institutional effectiveness in controlling stationary sources in period i

s_i = combustion processes at stationary sources in period i

l_i = institutional effectiveness in controlling mobile sources in period i

m_i = combustion processes at mobile sources in period i

w_i = meteorological conditions in period i

The estimatable function becomes

$$v_i = b_0 + b_s s_i w_i + b_m m_i w_i + b_g g_i t_i w_i \qquad (6\text{-}8)$$

where

$g_i t_i$ = either $s_i t_i$ (the time weight measure of stationary source activity) or $m_i t_i$ (the time weighted measure of mobile source activity)

b_g = either r_i (stationary source institutional effectiveness) or l_i (mobile source institutional effectiveness)

Notice should be taken that the meteorological condition is represented as a simple multiple of the relevant weight. In fact, the form of the meteorological weight is more complex. This is discussed and specified in the next section.

Even greater notice should be taken of the "either/or" form of the institutional factor. In essence, this form means that each model can be used to test two estimates of institutional effectiveness—one for mobile sources, with stationary source activity as background; another for the converse that tests stationary sources with mobile source activity as background. This "two-for-one" utilization of each model is reinforced by the adjustment for heteroskedasticity: when $s_i t$ (time weighted stationary source activity) is the variable used to estimate institutional effectiveness, then s_i (stationary source activity) is used as the heteroskedastic weight; when $m_i t$ (time weighted mobile sources) is the variable used to estimate institutional effectiveness, then m_i (mobile source activity) is used as the heteroskedastic weight.

This notational representation can be transformed into an estimateable function based on the work of Glen Cass and co-workers at the California Institute of Technology.[5] The actual functional specification by Cass was developed from hourly visibility data using the ambient concentration of sulfate, nitrate and the residual of ambient total suspended particulates as independent variables. The translation of the functional relationship to fit the annual data used for analysis here would be

$$v_i = b_0 + b_S SO_i (1-H_i)^{-\frac{2}{3}} + b_N NO_i (1-H_i)^{-\frac{2}{3}} + b_P TSP_i (1-H_i)^{-\frac{2}{3}} \quad \text{(6-9)}$$

where

SO_i =   ambient concentration of oxides of sulphur in period i

NO_i =   ambient concentration of oxides of nitrogen in period i

TSP_i =   ambient concentration of total suspended particulate minus the ambient concentration of oxides of sulphur and nitrogen in period i

H_i =   relative humidity in period i

    The coefficients in this estimator are estimates of the physical relationships between visibility reduction and the ambient concentrations specified. Since institutional activity is focused on source activity, the desired model must transform the estimators in equation (6-10)—which are based on physical relationships—into estimators based on source activity. The concentrations of these variables can be related to source activity by assuming that there is a constant per unit relationship between source activity and ambient effluent concentration. These constants will later become the terms for analyzing institutional effectiveness. On this basis, the ambient concentrations can be expressed as

$$SO_i = \frac{SO}{S}s_i + \frac{SO}{M}m_i \qquad (6\text{-}10)$$

$$NO_i = \frac{NO}{S}s_i + \frac{NO}{M}m_i \qquad (6\text{-}11)$$

$$TSP_i = \frac{TSP}{S}s_i + \frac{TSP}{M}m_i \qquad (6\text{-}12)$$

Where

$\dfrac{SO}{S}$ = ambient concentration of oxides of sulphur per unit of stationary source activity

$\dfrac{SO}{N}$ = ambient concentration of oxides of sulphur per unit of mobile source activity

$\dfrac{NO}{S}$ = ambient concentration of oxides of nitrogen per unit of stationary source activity

$\dfrac{NO}{M}$ = ambient concentration of oxides of nitrogen per unit of mobile source activity

$\dfrac{TSP}{S}$ = ambient concentration of total suspended particulate net of oxides of sulphur and nitrogen per unit of stationary source activity

$\dfrac{TSP}{M}$ = ambient concentration of total suspended particulate net of oxides of sulphur and nitrogen per unit of mobile source activity

Equation (6-10) can be reduced and simplified to

$$v_i = b_0 + b_s s_i (1 - H_i)^{-\frac{2}{3}} + b_m m_i (1 - H_i)^{-\frac{2}{3}} \qquad\qquad (6\text{-}13)$$

where

$$b_s = b_S \frac{SO}{S} + b_N \frac{NO}{S} + b_P \frac{TSP}{S}$$

and

$$b_m = b_S \frac{SO}{M} + b_N \frac{NO}{M} + b_P \frac{TSP}{M}$$

STRUCTURAL CHANGE

The basic causal model can now be specified by combining the results of the preceding section with the model introduced at the beginning of the previous chapter. The following section specifies the model; the second section discusses the choice of independent variables used and the tests performed; the final section discusses the results.

The causal model modifies the specification found in the previous chapter by introducing two independent measures of source activity and adjusting these for meteorological conditions. As the previous discussion indicates, doing so is appropriate for both institutional and technical reasons. The specifications from the previous chapter are repeated here, with modifications appropriate to the Cass Model discussed above. Once again, in these specifications the following conventions will be used

d_i $\begin{cases} = 1 \ \textit{for piece i} \\ = 0 \ \textit{for all other pieces} \end{cases}$

t = serial year

H = relative humidity

w = factor for meteorological conditions

= $(1-H)^{-\frac{2}{3}}$

E_T = total employment

E_M = manufacturing employment

S = stationary source activity weighted by meteorological activity

= $E_T w$ or $E_M w$

$S(i)$ = stationary source activity for piece i (from knot $i\text{-}1$ to knot i)

= $S - S_{knot\ i\text{-}1}$

V_T = total number of register vehicles

V_P = number of registered personal automobiles

M = mobile source activity weighted by meteorological activity

= $V_T w$ or $V_P w$

$M(i)$ = mobile source activity for piece i (from knot i-1 to knot i)

= $M - M_{knot\ i\text{-}1}$

R = institutional variable

= St or Mt

$R(i)$ = institutional variable for piece i (from *knot i-1* to knot i)

   = source activity weighted by serial year

   = $R - R_{knot\ i-1}$

Bi_j = coefficient for i^{th} piece of the jth independent variable, where j takes values S (stationary source activity), M (mobile source activity) or R (institutional variable)

$$= bi_j + \sum_{k=1}^{i-1} b(k)_j$$

The one-piece causal model is

$$v = bl_0 + bl_S S(1) + bl_M M(1) \tag{6-14}$$

The two-piece causal model is

$$v = bl_0 + bl_S S(1) + bl_M M(1) + B2_S S(2) \tag{6-15}$$

or

$$v = bl_0 + bl_S S(1) + bl_M M(1) + B2_M M(2) \tag{6-16}$$

The three-piece causal model is

$$v = bl_0 + bl_S S(1) + bl_M M(1) + B2_S S(2) + B3_S S(3) \tag{6-17}$$

or

$$v = bl_0 + bl_S S(1) + bl_M M(1) + B2_M M(2) + B3_M M(3) \tag{6-18}$$

The one-piece institutional model is

$$v = bl_0 + bl_S S(1) + bl_M M(1) + bl_R R(1) \tag{6-19}$$

The two-piece institutional model is

$$v = bl_0 + bl_S S(1) + bl_M M(1) + bl_R R(1) + B2_R R(2) \qquad \text{(6-20)}$$

The three-piece institutional model is

$$v = bl_0 + bl_S S(1) + bl_M M(1) + bl_R R(1) + B2_R R(2) + B3_R R(3) \qquad \text{(6-21)}$$

The first thing to notice about the independent variables specified for the equations above is that they are relatively unrelated to combustion—especially fuel use. There are two basic reasons for selecting these as the independent variables.[6]

The first reason for using these measures is practical: both of these variables are direct, annual measures. Fuel consumption for stationary sources and vehicle miles travelled for mobile sources must not only be derived from other data, but annual estimates must be interpolated from periodic survey data. This latter especially could lead to spurious results arising from seemingly significant knots resulting from these interpolations rather than the data they are intended to scale up.

The second reason for using these measures is theoretical: employment decisions and vehicle registrations are systematically related to effluent production but are at a distance from it. Once again, the analytic motive is to capture in the "institutional" variable the effect of decisionmaking that affects the relevant part of the combustion process.

The second major feature of the independent variables used is that each source type has associated with it two measures. Employment is measured for manufacturing only and for all employment: the former focusing on the most identifiably polluting sector; the latter focusing on the general level of economic activity. Vehicle registrations are measured for personal vehicles and for the total of personal and commercial vehicles[7]: the former associated with Southern California's alleged "love affair" with the automobile[8]; the latter associated more strongly with general economic activity.

This twofold measure for each source type means that each model can be tested two ways—one combination uses manufacturing and all vehicle registrations; the second combination uses total employment and personal automobile registrations.[9] In addition, each of these two can be tested twice: once using the mobile source utilized (i.e., either all vehicle registrations or personal automobile registrations) to adjust for heteroskedasticity and to create the "institutional" variable; and another time using the stationary variable (i.e., manufacturing employment or total employment) for these purposes.

The final feature of the data used as the independent variables is that they are county specific. Historically a major complaint of non-Los Angeles counties—particularly Riverside and San Bernardino—has been that they are victims of Los Angeles and Orange county source activity. This complaint is tested for: Long Beach is tested against Los Angeles and Orange county data; Riverside is tested against Los Angeles, Orange and Riverside/San Bernardino county data; and San Bernardino is tested against Los Angeles and Riverside/San Bernardino data.

The basic hypothesis brought to the analysis of this data is that source activity adjusted for the response of superstructural institutions will be adequate to explain "what happened." This means that the explanation of the trend in visibility reduction when tested against source activity will not be improved on by the use of a piecewise model used to model structural change. The method used here therefore is to select the best institutional model—i.e., including both source activity variables and institutional variables as regressors—and determine if the piecewise model provides an explanation that is better than the one-piece institutional model.

The results summarized in Table 6-IV, Table 6-V and Table 6-VI below are intended to provide the best estimates of the relationship between source activity and visibility reduction. In all cases the relationship between source activity and visibility reduction should be positive: increases in activity positively correlated with worsening of visibility. Thus the factors $S(1)$ (stationary source) and $M(1)$ (mobile source activity) should be positive for all series except the Downtown Average Daily Minimum Visibility series, where an increase in the dependent variable indicates visibility improvement. Likewise with the "institutional" variable: for all series except the Downtown Average Daily Minimum Visibility series, a positive coefficient indicates worsening of visibility.

Emphasis should be placed on the correct interpretation of the "institutional" variable for the second piece in the estimates that test for structural change. These coefficients—i.e., $B2$ and $B3$—are net coefficients. That is, this coefficient records the change from the coefficient given for the first piece not the absolute value of this factor. Thus if $b1 = -2.0$ (i.e., improvement) and $B2 = -1.0$ (i.e., improvement), it means that worsening over the previous piece has occurred but that the net effect has not been sufficient for an absolute worsening of visibility.[10]

Table 6-IV

Best institutional models for estimating of visibility data, 1950-82

Location	County Source Activity	Mobile Source (Vehicles)	Stationary Source (Employment)	Institutional Variable
Downtown Los Angeles				
Average Minimum	Los Angeles	Personal	Total	Total
< 3 Miles	Los Angeles	Personal	Total	Personal Autos
< 7 Miles	Los Angeles	All	Total	All Vehicles
Los Angeles International Airport				
< 7 Miles (FAA)	Los Angeles	All	Total	All Vehicles
< 3 Miles (FAA)	Los Angeles	Personal	Total	Personal Autos
< 3 Miles (Keith)	Los Angeles	Personal	Total	Personal Autos
Burbank	Los Angeles	All	Total	All Vehicles
Long Beach	Orange	All	Total	All Vehicles
Riverside	Orange	All	Total	All Vehicles
San Bernardino	Riverside/San Bernardino	All	Manufacturing	Manufacturing Employment

Table 6-IV shows how the addition of the institutional variable *R(1)* improves the estimate of the trend. These models establish a number of characteristics between air quality and the underlying technical and institutional causes of air quality reduction and improvement: mobile source activity appears to be heavily implicated in explaining the variation in visibility; the effect of institutional intervention has been generally positive; although Riverside appears to be a victim of Orange County effluents, San Bernardino appears to be a victim of Kaiser Steel which has dominated San Bernardino County manufacturing and employment generally.

Table 6-V provides the results from the piecewise models that show improvement over the one-piece institutional model. Only three locations show unambiguous improvement over the one-piece model: the Keith Study Los Angeles International Airport data; the Burbank data; and the San Bernardino data. However, very little changes in these models. The San Bernardino model further implicates the role of

Table 6-V

Piecewise models that improve over the best one-piece institutional model

Location	Knots		Effect on Trend from Use of Institutional Variable	Change in		
	1st	2nd		County	Source	Institutional Variable
LAX (Keith)	1960	1974	Improve (1950-60) Worsen (1960-74) Worsen (1974-82)	No	No	No
Burbank	1960	1968	Improve (1950-60) Worsen (1960-68) Improve (1968-82	No	No	No
San Bernardino	1968	1974	Improve (1950-68) Worsen (1968-74) Improve (1974-82)	No	No	Yes (to Manufacturing employment)

Kaiser Steel by the shift from mobile to stationary source activity as the strongest heteroskedastic weight and institutional variable; this is re-enforced by the location of the terminal knot at 1974 resulting in a shift from worsening to improvement in the institutional variable—a time when Kaiser Steel began its decline into an eventual shutdown and when SCAQMD began operation shortly thereafter. Nothing more occurs in the Burbank model than a worsening in the mid-1960s. This is potentially explicable by the influx of population and industry into the San Fernando Valley in the 1960s. The Keith Study results are somewhat anomalous because they are not matched by the FAA results. Once again the location of the knots implicate the influx of industry into the area in the 1960s.

The results of the analysis of the long term (1933-1979) downtown Los Angeles data are not sustained in the fully specified model. The implication is that this full specification is adequate in explaining what happened without the introduction of a control for structural change. What is most significant about these results is that no general improvement occurs from the application of piecewise models to the data. Moreover, the implication from the best models (whether piecewise or one-piece) is that the general institutional impact has been positive. A further implication is that mobile source activity is most heavily implicated for explaining the variation in visibility: eight of the ten models show the best results when the heteroskedastic weight and basis for the institutional variable is the mobile source activity.

However, the comparison of coefficients for each source activity as

Table 6-VI

Magnitude of mobile and stationary source coefficients

Location Dependent Variable	Variable for Source Activity			
	Mobile (M)		Stationary (S)	
	Coefficient	t-Statistic	Coefficient	t-Statistic
Downtown Los Angeles				
< 3 Miles	-5.0	-0.9	10.3	1.5
< 7 Miles	6.0	1.8	28.4	2.1
Avg Min	-0.2	-0.6	-0.8	-1.1
Los Angeles International Airport				
< 3 Miles (Keith)	5.3	1.8	1.5	0.5
< 3 Miles (FAA)	-0.3	-0.2	3.4	1.8
< 7 Miles (FAA)	1.7	0.6	10.3	0.9
Burbank	4.7	1.1	9.6	0.7
Long Beach	9.2	0.8	7.8	0.2
Riverside	23.6	1.8	30.4	0.5
San Bernardino	2.8	0.1	600.7	2.1

shown in Table 6-VI indicates that emphasis needs to be placed on the idea that the *variation* is most powerfully explained by mobile source activity: in eight of the ten models the impact of the stationary source is greater than that for the mobile source; in seven cases the impact is greater by a factor of at least two.[11]

SUMMARY AND CONCLUSION

Although analysis of the air quality data by itself indicated structural change, control for the underlying causal and institutional factors that contribute to air quality improvement and deterioration was able to explain the majority of these apparent structural shifts.

The primary conclusion, is therefore that a supply/demand model does not explain what happened to air quality in Southern California. Since incrementalism is the hallmark of supply/demand models, such a conclusion should appear to be counter-intuitive. A brief review of the argument is therefore worthwhile.

The basic utilitarian market model is that incremental change occurs because of decisions at the margin. These marginal adjustments assume a set of market rules. One kind of incrementalist picture of regulatory institutions portrays the political marketplace as affording little availability for anything other than incremental change (e.g., the concept of exfoliation). These models almost exclusively take political institutions as somehow exceptionally rigid and somehow external to the relevant institutional process—as somehow not subject to the rules of the game.

This appears as a kind of cynicism resulting, ironically, from a naivete about how political institutions are "supposed" to work. Creation of a regulatory institution is "supposed" to result in dramatic changes in the thing that is being regulated; regulators are given their mandate, which they thereupon are expected to relentlessly pursue. Historically the institutions that have affected air quality in Southern California have experienced some dramatic changes in the rules of the game—changes comparable to a shift in the supply of and demand for air quality. If political institutions are thought of as marketplaces where trade-offs are made, where equilibria are sought under a given set of market rules and where equilibria are incrementally found when the rules of the game change, then the lack of dramatic change makes perfect sense. Subtle change is something altogether different.

A change in the supply or demand function means a search for a new equilibrium, which should be evidenced by a shift in the behavior of the thing affected. Ordinarily, the result is a change in price and quantity. The econometrics of structural change was developed so these kinds of shifts could be detected. The rules of the environmental control game appear to have changed from what they were before World War II. However, when the data are controlled for the underlying source activity, the institutional impact has been seamless.

The functionalist theory is intended to explain this uniformity. Incrementalism remains relevant as does the idea that changes in the rules of the game will show up in the trend in real variables. The functionalist conception is integrative: air pollution institutions are of a piece with other superstructural institutions; in their turn superstructural institutions develop in response to the needs of the more fundamental political economy. The rules of the game are defined by this political economy and not by the conditions under which individuals can bargain over the supply of clean air. The political economy of smog has been the political economy of Southern California. The rules of that latter game have not changed.

NOTES

1. Primary pollutants are those effluents, such as reactive hydrocarbons, which are regulated.

2. The most infamous and damaging form of atmospheric sulphate is hydrogen sulphate—sulphuric acid, the first identified form of acid rain. The infamy of sulphuric acid results from its being the first identifiable cause of acid rain.

3. Like sulphate, nitrate forms an acid—nitric acid—which contributes to acid rain. Until recently acid rain was associated with sulphuric acid produced from the burning of coal. In the United States, acid rain was therefore thought to be an East Coast phenomenon because virtually no coal is burned on the West Coast. However, researchers at the California Institute of Technology have identified a related phenomenon: acid precipitation. The active ingredient of these acid fogs is nitric acid.

4. Cass, Boone and Macias [1981].

5. Cass [1979].

6. Other variables were used as preliminary estimators of source activity--namely, an estimate of fuel use by stationary sources and vehicle miles travelled by mobile sources and per capita values for employment, registrations, fuel use and vehicle miles travelled.

7. Survey data on vehicle miles travelled compiled by the Los Angeles Area Region Transportation Study (LAARTS) generally show that commercial utilization per vehicle is about twice that for personal vehicle use.

8. Even though, once again according to LAARTS surveys, the ratio of work related to non-work related vehicle miles travelled per vehicle is about 1 to 1.

9. The other two logical possibilities will tend to either over- or under-count activity. For example, commercial vehicle use would be counted in the transportation industry, so that total employment (including employment in the transportation industry) indirectly counts this source activity.

10. The appropriate arithmetic is

    $B2_R = b2_R + b1_R$

    or

    $b2_R$ = coefficient for the second piece $R(2)$

    $\quad\ = B2_R - b1_R$

    With

    $B2_R = -1.0$

    and

    $b1_R = -2.0$

    it follows that

    $b2_R = +1.0$

    which indicates worsening over the period covered by $R(2)$.

11. This is, of course, a tricky comparison. The two independent variables measure two very different things. However, the variables were scaled so that the magnitudes would be within approximately the same range: so that employment is measured in hundred-thousands employed; registrations in millions registered. As it turns out, if the regressions are performed using the source activity as a percent of the first year (i.e., indexed) the results are similar to those presented here.

REFERENCES

Barone, J.B., et al. 1978. A multivariate statistical analysis of visibility degradation at four California cities. *Atmospheric environments.* 12 (1978), 2213-2221.

California State Department of the Highway Patrol. Annual statistical report.

California State Department of Transportation. Registered autos and trucks for California.

California State Department of Finance. *California fact book.*

Cass, Glen. 1976. The relationship between sulfate air quality and visibility at Los Angeles. *California Institute of Technology Environmental Quality Laboratory Memorandum No. 18.* (August, 1976).

Cass, Glen, et al. 1981. Wintertime carbonaceous aerosols in Los Angeles: an exploration of the role of elemental carbon. *American Chemical Society Symposium Series 167.*

Cass, Glen. 1979. On the relationship between sulfate air quality and visibility with examples in Los Angeles. *Atmospheric environments.* 13 (1979), 1069-1084.

Keith, Ralph. 1979. Low visibility trends in the South Coast Air Basin (1950-1977). *South Coast Air Quality Management District.* (January, 1979).

Kidner, Frank L. and Neff, Phillip. 1945. *A statistical appendix to* An economic survey of the Los Angeles area. Los Angeles: The Haynes Foundation.

Leaderer, Brian, Holford, Theodore and Stolwijk, Jan. 1979. Relationship between sulfate aerosol and visibility. *Journal of the Air Pollution Control Association.* 29:2 (January, 1979), 154-157.

Los Angeles Regional Transportation Study. 1971. 1967 origin-destination survey. (December, 1971).

Los Angeles Regional Transportation Study. 1963. Base year report 1960. (December, 1963).

Trijonis, John. 1979. Visibility in the Southwest--an exploration of the historial data base. *Atmospheric environments.* 13 (1979), 833-843.

Trijonis, John, et al. 1976. Emissions and air quality trends in the South Coast Air Basin. *California Institute of Technology Environmental Quality Laboratory Memorandum No. 16.* (January, 1976).

U.S. Department of Labor, Bureau of Labor Statistics. *Employment and earnings.*

White, Warren H. and Roberts, P.T. 1977. On the nature and origins of visibility-reducing aerosols in the Los Angeles Air Basin. *Atmospheric environments.* 11 (1977), 803-812.

White, Warren H. and Husar, Rudolf B. 1976. A lagrangian model of the Los Angeles smog aerosol. *Journal of the Air Pollution Control Association.* 26:1 (January, 1976), 32-35.

CHAPTER 7

Conclusion

...this most excellent canopy, the air, look you, this brave
o'erhanging firmament, this majestical roof fretted with golden
fir, why, it appeareth nothing to me but a foul and pestilent
congregation of vapors. What piece of work is a man, how
noble in reason, how infinite in faculties.... (*Hamlet*, II,ii)

Environmental activists are utopians. They want a social system
unlike the one they live in—a society with an environmentally benign
mode of production. Environmentalists focus their attention and actions
on alternative ways of providing material needs, and on alternative
material needs per se. Their challenge to the status quo is one the most
potentially revolutionary an industrial society can face: how to socially
control production and how to create institutions in which individuals
have interests that do not inflict harm on others nor on the natural
environment which sustains us all.

In his recent book, *Making Peace with the Planet*[1], Barry
Commoner argues that in the last twenty years virtually no
improvement in environmental quality has occurred. Neither the
ascendancy of the environmentalist movement, the passage of sweeping
legislation nor the expenditure of vast sums of money have
accomplished anything more than tread environmental water. He argues
that the reason for this stagnation is that the real cause of

179

environmental degradation has not been addressed: namely, that the power to decide what technologies will be developed and deployed is held by an economic elite whose objectives have nothing to do with environmental improvement. This conclusion is one espoused in the present study and supported by its findings. The present study concludes that none of the dramatic institutional changes that have occurred during the history of smog in Southern California has resulted in a dramatic shift in air quality. The implication of this finding is that the kinds of institutional change which have occurred are not the right kind to cause the change required to achieve the environmental improvements sought by environmentalists.

That the institutional change which occurred did not translate into a shift in air quality improvement is only half the story. If the result implies that these institutional changes were not of the right kind, then what institutional changes are of the right kind? More to the point, what explains the ineffectiveness of what was done? In looking for an explanation I evaluated two political economic models of institutional structure and change: what I referred to as the utilitarian and functionalist models. The utilitarian model is associated with mainstream, neoclassical applied microeconomic and public choice theory. The functionalist model is associated with dissenting traditions in economics, particularly institutionalist and marxist political economics.

The utilitarian model portrays mainstream political economic thought by representing actions taken on environmental issues as a set of bargains struck among the actors in the theatre of public affairs. The four features of environmental politics were represented in the model: citizen activism, seemingly unresponsive bureaucracies, normative conflict and exfoliation of knowledge about environmental degradation. The model was used to identify what should count from the mainstream economic perspective as structural change in air pollution control—structural change that would cause a shift in the quality of the air.

The vision behind the utilitarian model and the mainstream political economics it represents is an image of human relations reduced to the exchange relations of the market. We can therefore talk meaningfully of the supply and demand for clean air. Maintaining the market analogy, we can also talk of shifts in the supply and demand functions which describe, for example, the willingness of citizens to demand cleaner air. These shifts in the supply and demand for clean air should cause a corresponding shift in the cleanliness of the air itself.

The history of air pollution control in Southern California was examined and revealed a number of periods during which substantial institutional change occurred. In the 1940s, air pollution reached the political agenda, the decade concluding with the creation of the first modern air pollution control agency, the Los Angeles County Air Pollution Control District. In the 1950s the role of the automobile in creating air pollution was revealed, along with the photochemical reactions which linked the automobile to smog. By the end of the decade, the responsibility for stationary sources was isolated from mobile sources. Originally the local agency had jurisdiction over both sources. In the late 1950s the state, in the form of the California Motor Vehicle Pollution Control Board, took over jurisdiction for mobile sources, leaving the local agency with responsibility for stationary sources. In the 1960s the federal government took responsibility for mobile source regulation. At the same time, the federal government intervened in stationary source control by establishing uniform national standards along with state and local planning requirements to meet those standards.

Except for the initial agitation leading up to the creation of the Los Angeles Air Pollution Control District, citizen activism throughout the 1940s and 1950s focused primarily on supporting the efforts of the local agency. However, with the rise of the environmental movement in the 1960s and the perceived lack of progress in eliminating smog, citizen activism turned against the local air pollution regulators. And in the mid-1970s, in the wake of both the shift in citizen activism and intervention by the state and federal governments, local air pollution control was dramatically reorganized with the creation of the South Coast Air Quality Control District.

The quantitative analysis in the last three chapters looked at visibility trends to see whether these dramatic institutional changes resulted in a corresponding shift in the improvement of air quality. Three facts were revealed. First, the incidence of severe visibility reduction in the South Coast Air Basin has generally improved, although in most cases at a diminishing rate. Second, at a limited number of sites—four out of the ten locations examined—estimates of visibility trends improved when structural change was built into the econometric model. Third, when the estimates of visibility trends are controlled for underlying stationary and mobile source activity, the number of sites showing structural change was further reduced to three out of ten locations.

The utilitarian model does not explain this basic stability amidst change. The functionalist model does explain this stability because the function of air pollution regulation is not to improve air quality. Rather, air pollution regulation is intended to prevent the clean air issue from interfering with the accumulation of capital and the power of the capitalist class over production decisions. This view is consistent with the broader view of government and other non-economic institutions as superstructural. Such superstructural institutions support and are necessary for maintaining the basic economic relations which are the necessary conditions for capitalist accumulation. However, these superstructural institutions are not themselves essential for accumulation. Superstructural institutions provide their essential supporting role through three dimensions of power in which the interests of the capitalist class prevail.

These three dimensions of power describe how the interests of one group prevail when those interests are in conflict with the interests of another group. The first dimension of power is the ability to prevail in a decision which is on the political or other public agenda. The second dimension of power is the ability to prevent issues involving a conflict of interest from reaching an appropriate agenda. The third dimension of power covers those instances when the interests of one group prevail without that group taking any overt action at all. The third dimension is referred to as hegemonic power.

The supply and demand for clean air described by the exchange relations of the utilitarian model accounts for only two of the three dimensions in which power is exercised by the capitalist class. None of the dramatic changes examined challenge, nor could they be expected to challenge, the preemptive power of business to select and deploy technologies, regardless of the broader impact of those technologies. This lack of challenge is exemplified by the preponderance of air pollution control which has focused on technologies that work on what comes out of the tailpipe or smokestack. Requirements to use the best available control technology (BACT), incorporated early on in air pollution policy, embody these limitations. The emphasis is on control of effluents, not prevention of effluents.

The function of air pollution control to abate interference with capitalist accumulation is fulfilled in two broad ways. First, the interests of business are at a huge advantage in their ability to excercise the first and second dimensions of power—business interests have vastly greater resources to throw at environmental issues. Second and more important, the hegemonic power of the capitalist class ensures that the social roles which people fulfill systematically avoid a challenge to capitalist dominance. That hegemony arises from the ecology of institutional roles.

Business decisionmakers may care about the quality of the environment in their personal life, but when they are on the job they cannot concern themselves with the environment nearly as much as they must concern themselves with the accumulation of capital. That is what they are supposed to do—make money, and ensure the success and growth of the company. Regulators want to do a good job by improving environmental quality, but not by violating the rights that place the power over the production process in the hands of private decisionmakers. Regulators are not supposed to put people out of business; they are supposed to serve all interests in the community, including business interests. On the other hand, environmentalists want an institutional environment that will improve environmental quality, but they also want to be politically effective within the existing institutional framework. They are supposed to be realistic and responsible about their demands; responsible environmentalists are supposed to settle for small victories rather than pursue glorious and principled defeats.

The very least that can be said is that deterioration can be prevented. The converse to Commoner's despair over the lack of environmental improvement is that without the efforts that were made, environmental degradation would have been the norm. Environmentalist efforts have been effective in holding the otherwise downward spiral of environmental decay.

If the framework for reform remains within capitalist institutions, perhaps creating market mechanisms to achieve environmental ends is in fact the most that can be hoped for. However, Bruce Yandle, a true believer in the use of market based mechanisms for achieving environmental goals, despairs of their ever being effective.[2] His reason is illuminating. The act of setting policy and implementing it is subject to bargaining between polluters and environmentalists. Compromise is inevitable. In the end, it is not the tool which is important but the will and ability, as defined by the institutional environment, to use the tool.

To understand how environmentalist goals can be achieved, we need to look again at the four features of environmental politics. In particular, we should look a the normative conflict involved in environmental decisionmaking. In principle, capitalist institutions can support environmental improvement. The reason, strangely enough, is that the general conditions for environmental improvement have nothing which is in direct conflict with capitalist accumulation. Production in capitalist society is the production of exchange values rather than of use values. Exchange value is the value a thing has in the market; use value is the value a thing has in satisfying some need or want. The institutional arrangements required for environmental improvement in a capitalist society are those which will exercise the imagination of businesses so they will create only those exchange values which are environmentally sane and which are produced with technologies that are environmentally benign.

Good luck.

In the absence of a massive environmental awakening by the business elite, hope must center on reforms that increase the power of people to recognize and act on their environmental interests. One family of reforms should bring economies to environmental activism, for instance by creating funded positions within environmental agencies for environmental advocates—people whose job it is to be a resource to environmentalists. Another sort of reform should fund community organizers to work with communities on environmental issues. A second family of reforms should link environmentalism to the redistribution of income. To paraphrase Bertolt Brecht, first a decent living and then a clean environment. As argued in Chapter 2, and more fully discussed by Hays[3], environmentalism arose after World War II in association with rising incomes. Rising incomes led to an increase in both the ability and willingness to demand a higher quality of life. Eliminating poverty and promoting a high quality of life will inevitably increase the demand for environmental improvement.

One of the limits to focusing on environmental activism is that, although it has been the driving force behind the environmental movement, it focuses on local rather than regional or national concerns. Barry Commoner proposes that decisions regarding the development and use of technologies be subject to substantial social control. To be effective, the institutions responsible for that control will have to be moved into action by a sustained environmental activism. Such a level of activism, although possible, is not characteristic of the activism discussed as a feature of environmental politics. This latter activism has been in response to degradation in the local quality of life. For Commoner's proposal to work, institutional mechanisms must be created to provide the intensity of activism at this higher level which characterizes the environmental concern for the quality of life in the activists' local community. Dramatic change is required. A dramatic change in the rules of the game, rules of environmentalist's making.

The history of air pollution control and institutional change in Southern California tells us that environmentalists, in order to be effective, must play by the rules. But the rules which define the political economy of smog in Southern California are currently made outside any forum where environmental values can be incorporated into basic decisions about the production process. The rhythm of air pollution control in Southern California has the meter of its economic base: the political economy of smog in Southern California is the political economy of growth.

And the band plays on.

NOTES

1. Commoner [1990].

2. Yandle [1989].

3. Hays [1987].

REFERENCES

Commoner, Barry. 1990. *Making peace with the planet*. New York: Pantheon.

Hays, Samuel P. 1987. *Beauty, health, and permanence: environmental politics in the United States, 1955-1985*. Cambridge: Cambridge.

Yandle, Bruce. 1989. *The political limits of environmental regulation: tracking the unicorn*. New York: Quorum.

APPENDICES

APPENDIX A

Graphs of Visibility Data
with Linear Estimators

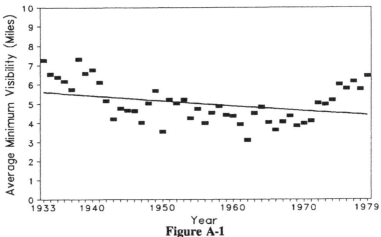

Figure A-1
Downtown Los Angeles, 1933-1979
Average Minimum Daily Visibility

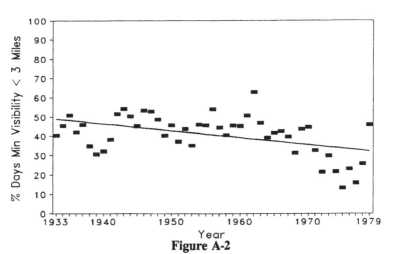

Figure A-2
Downtown Los Angeles, 1933-1979
Percent Days Minimum Daily Visibility Less Than 3 Miles

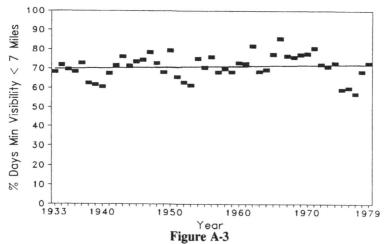

Figure A-3
Downtown Los Angeles, 1933-1979
Percent Days Minimum Daily Visibility Less Than 7 Miles

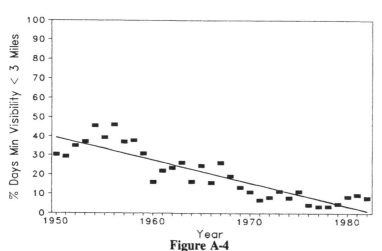

Figure A-4
Los Angeles International Airport, 1950-1982 (Keith)
Percent Days Minimum Daily Visibility Less Than 3 Miles

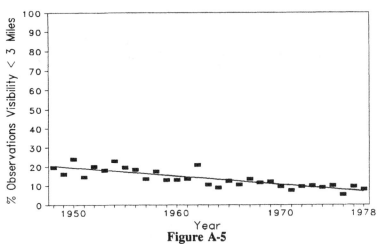

Figure A-5
Los Angeles International Airport, 1948-1978 (FAA)
Percent Observations Visibility Less Than 3 Miles

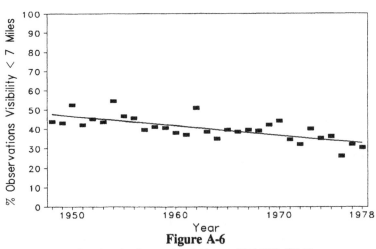

Figure A-6
Los Angeles International Airport, 1948-1978 (FAA)
Percent Observations Visibility Less Than 7 Miles

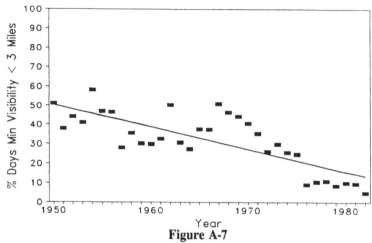

Figure A-7
Burbank Airport, 1950-1982
Percent Days Minimum Daily Visibility Less Than 3 Miles

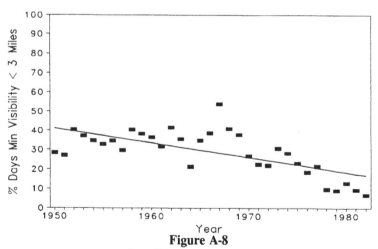

Figure A-8
Long Beach Airport, 1950-1982
Percent Days Minimum Daily Visibility Less Than 3 Miles

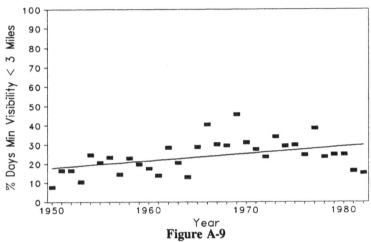

Figure A-9
Riverside (March Air Force Base), 1950-1982
Percent Days Minimum Daily Visibility Less Than 3 Miles

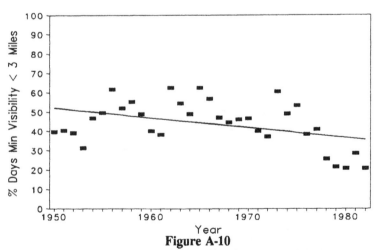

Figure A-10
San Bernardino (Norton Air Force Base), 1950-1982
Percent Days Minimum Daily Visibility Less Than 3 Miles

APPENDIX B
Graphs of Visibility Data
with Cubic Estimators

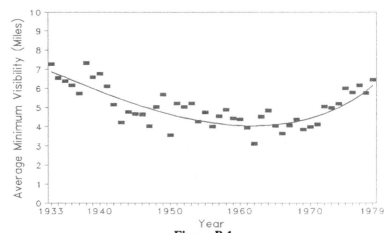

Figure B-1
Downtown Los Angeles, 1933-1979
Average Minimum Daily Visibility

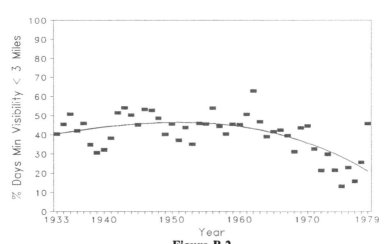

Figure B-2
Downtown Los Angeles, 1933-1979
Percent Days Minimum Daily Visibility Less Than 3 Miles

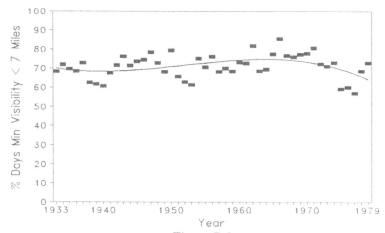

Figure B-3
Downtown Los Angeles, 1933-1979
Percent Days Minimum Daily Visibility Less Than 7 Miles

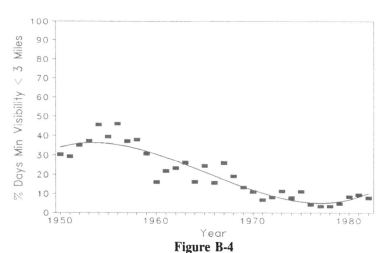

Figure B-4
Los Angeles International Airport, 1950-1982 (Keith)
Percent Days Minimum Daily Visibility Less Than 3 Miles

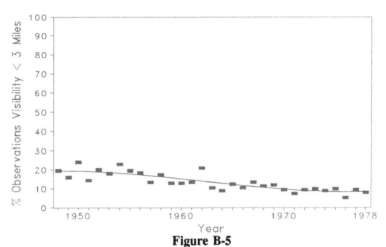

Figure B-5
Los Angeles International Airport, 1948-1978 (FAA)
Percent Observations Visibility Less Than 3 Miles

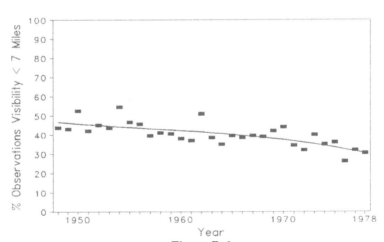

Figure B-6
Los Angeles International Airport, 1948-1978 (FAA)
Percent Observations Visibility Less Than 7 Miles

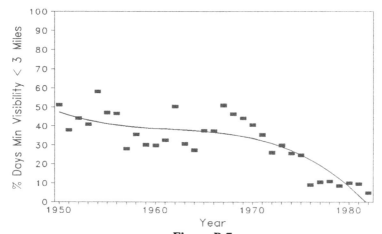

Figure B-7
Burbank Airport, 1950-1982
Percent Days Minimum Daily Visibility Less Than 3 Miles

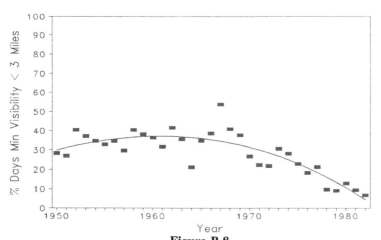

Figure B-8
Long Beach Airport, 1950-1982
Percent Days Minimum Daily Visibility Less Than 3 Miles

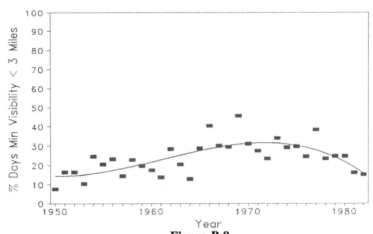

Figure B-9
Riverside (March Air Force Base), 1950-1982
Percent Days Minimum Daily Visibility Less Than 3 Miles

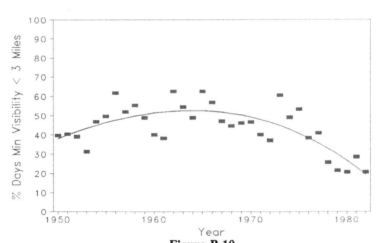

Figure B-10
San Bernardino (Norton Air Force Base), 1950-1982
Percent Days Minimum Daily Visibility Less Than 3 Miles

APPENDIX C
Visibility Data

Table C-I
Downtown Los Angeles, 1933-79

Year	Average Min Daily Visibility (Miles)	Percent Days Min Visibility < 3 Miles	Percent Days Min Visibility < 7 Miles	Year	Average Min Daily Visibility (Miles)	Percent Days Min Visibility < 3 Miles	Percent Days Min Visibility < 7 Miles
1933	7.27	40.35	68.26	1957	4.54	44.35	68.20
1934	6.54	45.42	71.89	1958	4.88	40.32	69.76
1935	6.39	50.70	69.58	1959	4.42	45.38	68.27
1936	6.16	42.04	68.51	1960	4.38	45.31	73.06
1937	5.72	45.85	72.86	1961	3.93	50.62	72.43
1938	7.31	34.94	62.40	1962	3.12	62.86	81.63
1939	6.57	30.62	61.58	1963	4.53	46.77	68.55
1940	6.76	32.14	60.62	1964	4.84	39.00	69.29
1941	6.11	38.28	67.49	1965	4.04	41.48	77.29
1942	5.14	51.40	71.54	1966	3.64	42.39	85.60
1943	4.21	54.15	76.09	1967	4.08	39.50	76.47
1944	4.75	50.22	71.37	1968	4.37	31.25	75.83
1945	4.66	45.15	73.58	1969	3.86	43.57	77.18
1946	4.65	53.20	74.37	1970	3.98	44.53	77.73
1947	4.02	52.72	78.39	1971	4.12	32.49	80.59
1948	5.03	48.66	72.74	1972	5.04	21.37	72.22
1949	5.68	40.29	68.13	1973	4.98	29.83	71.01
1950	3.55	45.57	79.32	1974	5.20	21.55	72.85
1951	5.21	37.14	65.71	1975	6.01	13.19	59.15
1952	5.03	43.67	62.86	1976	5.79	22.98	60.00
1953	5.21	35.10	61.22	1977	6.16	15.64	56.98
1954	4.25	45.97	75.00	1978	5.76	25.43	68.53
1955	4.74	45.49	70.49	1979	6.45	45.68	72.84
1956	4.00	53.88	75.92				

Table C-II
Keith Study, South Coast Air Basin, 1950-82

Year	LA International Airport	Burbank	Long Beach	Riverside	San Bernardino
1950	30.38	51.05	28.27	7.59	39.66
1951	29.39	37.96	26.94	16.33	40.41
1952	35.10	44.08	40.41	16.33	39.18
1953	37.14	40.82	37.14	10.20	31.43
1954	45.56	58.06	34.68	24.60	46.77
1955	39.34	47.13	32.79	20.49	49.59
1956	46.12	46.53	34.69	23.27	61.63
1957	37.24	28.03	29.71	14.23	51.88
1958	37.90	35.48	40.32	22.98	55.24
1959	30.92	30.12	38.15	19.68	49.00
1960	15.92	29.80	36.33	17.55	40.00
1961	21.81	32.51	31.69	13.58	38.27
1962	23.27	50.20	41.63	28.57	62.45
1963	26.21	30.65	35.48	20.56	54.44
1964	16.18	27.39	21.16	12.86	48.96
1965	24.45	37.55	34.93	28.82	62.45
1966	15.64	37.45	38.68	40.33	56.79
1967	26.05	50.84	53.78	30.25	47.06
1968	19.17	46.25	40.83	29.58	44.58
1969	13.28	43.98	37.76	45.64	46.06
1970	10.93	40.49	26.72	31.17	46.56
1971	6.75	35.44	22.36	27.43	40.08
1972	8.12	26.07	21.79	23.50	37.18
1973	11.34	29.83	30.67	34.03	60.50
1974	7.76	25.43	28.02	29.31	49.14
1975	11.06	24.68	22.98	29.79	53.19
1976	4.26	8.94	18.30	24.68	38.30
1977	3.40	10.21	21.28	38.30	40.85
1978	3.35	10.78	9.67	23.42	25.65
1979	4.85	8.48	9.09	24.85	21.52
1980	8.39	10.00	12.90	24.84	20.65
1981	9.51	9.51	9.51	16.14	28.53
1982	7.74	4.84	6.77	15.16	20.65

Table C-III

Federal Aviation Administration (FAA) Study LA International Airport, 1948-78

Year	Percent Min Observations < 3 Miles	Percent Min Observations < 7 Miles
1948	19.50	43.75
1949	16.00	43.00
1950	24.00	52.50
1951	14.50	42.00
1952	20.00	45.00
1953	18.00	43.50
1954	23.00	54.50
1955	19.50	46.50
1956	18.50	45.50
1957	13.50	39.50
1958	17.50	41.00
1959	13.00	40.50
1960	13.00	38.00
1961	13.50	37.00
1962	21.00	51.00
1963	10.50	38.50
1964	9.00	35.00
1965	12.25	39.50
1966	10.50	38.50
1967	13.50	39.50
1968	11.50	39.00
1969	12.00	42.00
1970	9.50	44.00
1971	7.50	34.50
1972	9.50	32.00
1973	10.00	40.00
1974	9.00	35.25
1975	10.00	36.25
1976	5.25	26.25
1977	9.50	32.00
1978	8.00	30.50

DATA SOURCE

Keith, Ralph. 1980. A climatological-air quality profile: California South Coast Air Basin. *South Coast Air Quality Management District.* (November, 1980).

Keith, Ralph. 1979. Low visibility trends in the South Coast Air Basin (1950-1977). *South Coast Air Quality Management District.* (January, 1979).

Keith, Ralph. 1970. Downtown Los Angeles noon visibility trends, 1933-1969. *Los Angeles Air Pollution Control District, Report No. 65.* (December 15, 1970).

Keith, Ralph. 1964. A study of low visibility trends in the Los Angeles Basin, 1950-1961. *Los Angeles Air Pollution Control District, Report No. 53.* (January, 1964).

U.S. Department of Transportation, Federal Aviation Administration. 1981. *Wind-ceiling-visibility data at selected airports.* (June, 1981).

APPENDIX D

Econometric Analysis of Visibility Trends

Table D-I

Comparison of Summary Statistics for
Cubic and Linear Estimates of Visibility Trends

Location and Variable Model	Functional Form	Adjusted R^2	Critical F Value	F Value For Model	Durban-Watson Statistic
Downtown LA	Cubic	.604	29.042	23.350	1.553
Average Minimum	Linear	.043	0.000	2.970	.632
Downtown LA	Cubic	.389	5.670	10.350	1.076
< 3 Miles	Linear	.220	0.000	13.410	.784
Downtown LA	Cubic	.123	3.156	3.060	1.279
< 7 Miles	Linear	-.012	0.000	.470	1.047
LAX (FAA)	Cubic	.676	-.270	20.450	2.417
< 3 Miles	Linear	.683	0.000	61.310	2.296
LAX (FAA)	Cubic	.528	0.000	11.420	2.176
< 7 Miles	Linear	.528	0.000	32.370	2.037
LAX (Keith)	Cubic	.838	5.460	56.050	1.354
< 3 Miles	Linear	.777	0.000	112.650	.966
Burbank	Cubic	.687	5.050	24.370	1.258
< 3 Miles	Linear	.578	0.000	44.820	.879
Long Beach	Cubic	.683	12.076	23.960	1.491
< 3 Miles	Linear	.419	0.000	24.070	.784
Riverside	Cubic	.462	8.301	10.140	2.089
< 3 Miles	Linear	.154	0.000	6.810	1.270
San Bernardino	Cubic	.544	12.592	13.700	1.580
< 3 Miles	Linear	.148	0.000	6.560	.813

Table D-II
Cubic and Linear Estimates of Visibility Trends
Downtown Los Angeles, 1933-79

Dependent Variable	Functional Form	Independent Variable	Coefficient	t-Statistic
Average Minimum	Cubic	CONSTANT	6.49092	19.480
		t1	-.12312	-1.856
		$t1^2$	-.00110	-.311
		$t1^3$	.00009	1.654
	Linear	CONSTANT	5.37144	19.449
		t1	-.01863	-1.723
< 3 Miles	Cubic	CONSTANT	40.06929	8.664
		t1	.80538	.875
		$t1^2$	-.02186	-.447
		$t1^3$	-.00014	-.189
	Linear	CONSTANT	49.29425	17.684
		t1	-.39957	-3.662
< 7 Miles	Cubic	CONSTANT	68.84178	20.884
		t1	-.32052	-.489
		$t1^2$	.04320	1.239
		$t1^3$	-.00087	-1.674
	Linear	CONSTANT	69.89406	37.005
		t1	.05051	.683

Table D-III

Cubic and Linear Estimates of Visiblity Trends
Los Angeles International Airport, 1948-78 (FAA) and 1950-82 (Keith)

Dependent Variable	Functional Form	Independent Variable	Coefficient	t-Statistic
< 3 Miles (FAA)	Cubic	CONSTANT	20.98053	11.478
		t1	-.62576	-1.087
		t1^2	-.00147	-.031
		t1^3	.00026	.233
	Linear	CONSTANT	20.02931	20.088
		t1	-.47869	-7.830
< 7 Miles (FAA)	Cubic	CONSTANT	49.65556	17.246
		t1	-1.57703	-1.740
		t1^2	-.00244	-1.367
		t1^3	.09869	1.299
	Linear	CONSTANT	47.72414	30.075
		t1	-.55357	-5.690
< 3 Miles (Keith)	Cubic	CONSTANT	34.05534	10.334
		t1	1.38113	1.525
		t1^2	-.22152	-3.338
		t1^3	.00484	3.554
	Linear	CONSTANT	39.46365	18.742
		t1	-1.20029	-10.614

Table D-IV

Cubic and Linear Estimates of Visibility Trends
Other Locations in the South Coast Air Basin, 1950-82

Location	Functional Form	Independent Variable	Coefficient	t-Statistic
Burbank	Cubic	CONSTANT	47.43309	9.278
		t1	-1.82569	-1.299
		$t1^2$	.13510	1.312
		$t1^3$	-.00393	-1.861
	Linear	CONSTANT	50.45269	15.592
		t1	-1.16352	-6.695
Long Beach	Cubic	CONSTANT	29.90548	7.614
		t1	1.30888	1.212
		$t1^2$	-.05481	-.693
		$t1^3$	-.00034	-.211
	Linear	CONSTANT	41.17562	14.202
		t1	-.76391	-4.906
Riverside	Cubic	CONSTANT	14.22655	3.578
		t1	-.06875	-.063
		$t1^2$	.11745	1.467
		$t1^3$	-.00355	-2.162
	Linear	CONSTANT	17.72257	6.518
		t1	.38112	2.610
San Bernardino	Cubic	CONSTANT	38.09418	7.633
		t1	1.93377	1.410
		$t1^2$	-.05232	-.521
		$t1^3$	-.00083	-.401
	Linear	CONSTANT	52.08562	14.007
		t1	-.51170	-2.562

APPENDIX E

Piecewise Cubic Estimates
of Visibility Trends

Table E-I

Comparison of Summary Statistics for Piecewise Cubic Models
Showing Improvement over the Base Cubic Model

Location and Variable Model	1st Knot	2nd Knot	Adjusted R^2	Critical F Value	F Value For Model	Durbin-Watson Statistic
Downtown LA < 7 Miles	1964	1974	.390	8.535	6.620	1.775
Downtown LA Average Minimum	1944	1956	.667	3.689	18.610	1.924
LAX (Keith) < 3 Miles	1960	1968	.883	5.192	49.300	2.025
	1960		.871	7.163	55.050	1.741
	1956		.858	3.944	49.420	1.665
Burbank (Keith) < 3 Miles	1960	1968	.794	7.012	25.690	2.056
	1960	1974	.768	4.713	22.160	1.839
	1956	1974	.756	3.818	20.780	1.801
	1964	1974	.752	3.538	20.370	1.705
	1956	1968	.749	3.335	20.060	1.773

Table E-II
Econometric Results for Downtown Los Angeles
Percent Days Minimum Visibility < 7 Miles

1st Knot	2nd Knot	Independent Variable	Coefficient	t-Statistic
1964	1974	CONSTANT	65.27367	21.327
		$t1$	1.33601	1.679
		$t1^2$	-.09886	-1.800
		$t1^3$	.00223	2.106
		$t2^3$	-.02457	-4.112
		$t3^3$	.24050	4.327

Table E-III
Econometric Results for Downtown Los Angeles
Average Minimum Daily Visibility

1st Knot	2nd Knot	Independent Variable	Coefficient	t-Statistic
1944	1956	CONSTANT	6.11070	13.139
		$t1$	.42708	1.403
		$t1^2$	-.11506	-2.224
		$t1^3$	.00602	2.416
		$t2^3$	-.00708	-2.529
		$t3^3$	.00160	3.122

Table E-IV
Econometric Results for
Los Angeles International Airport (Keith)
Percent Days Minimum Visibility < 3 Miles

1st Knot	2nd Knot	Independent Variable	Coefficient	t-Statistic
1960	1968	CONSTANT	25.22844	6.752
		t1	9.91444	4.014
		$t1^2$	-1.72607	-4.069
		$t1^3$	.07540	3.729
		$t2^3$	-.09286	-3.287
		$t3^3$	.02784	1.962
1960		CONSTANT	26.98508	7.086
		t1	7.31533	3.343
		$t1^2$	-1.16418	-3.544
		$t1^3$	.04565	3.251
		$t2^3$	-.04586	-2.917
1956		CONSTANT	26.66732	5.964
		t1	10.20218	2.575
		$t1^2$	-2.33263	-2.513
		$t1^3$	.15280	2.353
		$t2^3$	-.15055	-2.279

Table E-V

Econometric Results of Burbank Municipal Airport (Keith)
Percent Days Visibility < 3 Miles

1st Knot	2nd Knot	Independent Variable	Coefficient	t-Statistic
1960	1968	CONSTANT	42.89635	7.752
		$t1$	5.48922	1.501
		$t1^2$	-1.49153	-2.374
		$t1^3$	.08339	2.785
		$t2^3$	-.14045	-3.357
		$t3^3$	.08682	4.132
1960	1974	CONSTANT	45.10655	7.799
		$t1$	2.05879	.581
		$t1^2$	-.70891	-1.253
		$t1^3$	.03992	1.573
		$t2^3$	-.06249	-2.033
		$t3^3$	.10677	3.473
1956	1974	CONSTANT	44.75004	6.789
		$t1$	5.09258	.829
		$t1^2$	-1.98468	-1.326
		$t1^3$	.16033	1.500
		$t2^3$	-.17696	-1.606
		$t3^3$	.08769	3.189
1964	1974	CONSTANT	48.01663	8.627
		$t1$	-1.24520	-.460
		$t1^2$	-.05188	-.150
		$t1^3$	.00589	.481
		$t2^3$	-.03188	-1.454
		$t3^3$	.11143	2.836
1956	1968	CONSTANT	43.81200	6.511
		$t1$	7.99970	1.205
		$t1^2$	-2.98529	-1.759
		$t1^3$	.24387	1.957
		$t2^3$	-.27415	-2.084
		$t3^3$	.04988	3.024

APPENDIX F

Stationary and Mobile Source Activity Data

Table F-I

Los Angeles SMSA Manufacturing Employment, 1935-79

Year	Employment (00)	Year	Employment (00)
1935	946	1957	7,601
1936	1,104	1958	6,987
1937	1,292	1959	7,439
1938	1,164	1960	7,387
1939	1,279	1961	7,226
1940	1,535	1962	7,559
1941	2,251	1963	7,543
1942	3,312	1964	7,457
1943	4,392	1965	7,609
1944	4,174	1966	8,306
1945	3,477	1967	8,601
1946	3,111	1968	8,781
1947	3,533	1969	8,805
1948	3,764	1970	8,039
1949	3,763	1971	7,424
1950	4,145	1972	7,745
1951	4,979	1973	8,210
1952	5,773	1974	8,244
1953	6,261	1975	7,668
1954	6,266	1977	8,181
1955	6,786	1979	9,249
1956	7,321		

Table F-II
Los Angeles County Pollution Source Activity, 1950-82

Year	Stationary - Employment (00)		Mobile - Registered Vehicles (00,000)	
	Manufacturing	Total	Personal	Commercial
1950	4,145	14,152	17.18	1.60
1951	4,979	15,545	18.22	1.80
1952	5,773	16,743	18.98	1.93
1953	6,261	17,715	20.52	2.12
1954	6,266	17,880	21.48	2.28
1955	6,786	19,072	23.35	2.55
1956	7,321	20,299	24.33	2.73
1957	7,601	20,991	25.30	2.85
1958	6,987	20,377	26.16	3.05
1959	7,439	21,497	26.51	3.02
1960	7,387	21,893	27.81	3.14
1961	7,226	22,035	28.43	3.25
1962	7,559	22,948	30.32	3.68
1963	7,543	23,577	31.09	3.44
1964	7,457	24,151	32.31	3.90
1965	7,609	24,804	33.15	4.05
1966	8,306	26,205	33.65	4.20
1967	8,601	27,001	33.74	4.28
1968	8,781	27,961	35.38	4.57
1969	8,805	28,998	36.25	4.60
1970	8,039	28,598	36.70	4.77
1971	7,424	27,899	37.48	4.91
1972	7,745	28,881	37.98	5.10
1973	8,210	30,296	38.70	5.40
1974	8,244	30,737	38.22	6.26
1975	7,668	30,245	37.75	6.45
1976	7,899	31,072	39.22	6.81
1977	8,181	32,324	35.67	6.39
1978	8,779	34,306	36.23	6.65
1979	9,249	35,845	36.83	6.93
1980	9,160	36,202	37.36	7.32
1981	9,133	36,605	37.93	7.93
1982	8,628	35,407	38.50	7.95

Table F-III
Orange County Pollution Source Activity, 1950-82

Year	Stationary - Employment (00)		Mobile - Registered Vehicles (00,000)	
	Manufacturing	Total	Personal	Commercial
1950	79	466	0.93	0.10
1951	102	524	1.01	0.12
1952	123	578	1.06	0.13
1953	142	648	1.17	0.15
1954	147	685	1.28	0.16
1955	178	815	1.55	0.20
1956	226	976	1.85	0.23
1957	298	1,123	2.15	0.25
1958	334	1,250	2.46	0.29
1959	418	1,478	2.69	0.31
1960	474	1,658	3.11	0.35
1961	578	1,868	3.43	0.39
1962	775	2,212	3.96	0.48
1963	882	2,518	4.36	0.48
1964	918	2,756	4.89	0.58
1965	963	2,931	5.38	0.64
1966	1,078	3,242	5.77	0.70
1967	1,251	3,525	6.11	0.74
1968	1,289	3,801	6.69	0.81
1969	1,300	4,076	7.13	0.86
1970	1,236	4,206	7.48	0.95
1971	1,207	4,329	7.94	1.02
1972	1,325	4,738	8.47	1.14
1973	1,501	5,275	9.14	1.30
1974	1,586	5,592	9.20	1.66
1975	1,510	5,629	9.43	1.79
1976	1,613	6,103	9.50	1.78
1977	1,750	6,740	9.53	1.83
1978	1,980	7,477	9.90	1.96
1979	2,160	8,043	10.24	2.04
1980	2,205	8,364	10.74	2.16
1981	2,239	8,664	11.14	2.27
1982	2,124	8,488	11.56	2.39

Table F-IV
Riverside / San Bernardino County Pollution Source Activity, 1950-82

Year	Stationary - Employment (00)		Mobile - Registered Vehicles (00,000)	
	Manufacturing	Total	Personal	Commercial
1950	179	1,034	1.36	0.18
1951	214	1,172	1.45	0.20
1952	233	1,310	1.54	0.22
1953	282	1,388	1.69	0.25
1954	281	1,397	1.79	0.27
1955	301	1,509	1.98	0.30
1956	331	1,640	2.14	0.34
1957	358	1,781	2.27	0.37
1958	331	1,794	2.46	0.42
1959	346	1,862	2.51	0.43
1960	346	1,889	2.66	0.46
1961	346	1,922	2.75	0.49
1962	368	2,046	3.03	0.59
1963	379	2,171	3.42	0.55
1964	403	2,340	3.40	0.66
1965	421	2,442	3.62	0.71
1966	457	2,546	3.73	0.75
1967	474	2,595	3.78	0.76
1968	500	2,710	4.04	0.83
1969	533	2,874	4.20	0.84
1970	527	2,937	4.33	0.88
1971	521	2,989	4.52	0.93
1972	547	3,137	4.68	0.99
1973	580	3,297	4.86	1.07
1974	574	3,345	4.75	1.28
1975	511	3,330	4.80	1.37
1976	453	3,474	4.93	1.40
1977	585	3,749	4.94	1.46
1978	641	4,082	5.31	1.61
1979	674	4,298	5.60	1.74
1980	642	4,344	5.88	1.88
1981	629	4,379	6.19	2.02
1982	587	4,314	6.53	2.18

Table F-V
Average Annual Morning Relative Humidity
Los Angeles International Airport, 1950-82

Year	Relative Humidity (Percent)
1950	45.30
1951	44.80
1952	42.00
1953	37.80
1954	43.40
1955	42.30
1956	38.70
1957	40.70
1958	41.80
1959	42.70
1960	42.70
1961	41.70
1962	44.60
1963	40.00
1964	39.30
1965	44.90
1966	39.50
1967	44.70
1968	43.10
1969	38.20
1970	37.60
1971	43.30
1972	49.20
1973	46.80
1974	41.70
1975	41.10
1976	36.20
1977	42.70
1978	42.50
1979	42.80
1980	38.00
1981	43.00
1982	41.00

DATA SOURCE

California State Department of the Highway Patrol. Annual statistical report.

California State Department of Transportation. Registered autos and trucks for California.

California State Department of Finance. *California fact book.*

Kidner, Frank L. and Neff, Phillip. 1945. *A statistical appendix to* An economic survey of the Los Angeles area. Los Angeles: The Haynes Foundation.

U.S. Department of Labor, Bureau of Labor Statistics. *Employment and earnings.*

APPENDIX G
Institutional Models, Downtown Los Angeles
Visibility Data 1935-79

Table G-I
Comparison of Summary Statistics for
Institutional and Causal Model Downtown Los Angeles, 1935-79

Dependent Variable	Model	Adjusted R^2	Critical F Value	F Value for Model	Durban-Watson Statistic
Average	Institutional	.521	-31.040	24.900	1.239
Minimum	Causal	.875	0.000	.720	.544
< 3 Miles	Institutional	.396	-19.748	15.410	1.051
	Causal	.680	0.000	3.710	.735
< 7 Miles	Institutional	.053	-40.359	2.240	1.146
	Causal	.963	0.000	.650	.963

Table G-II
Institutional and Causal Model for Downtown Los Angeles, 1935-79

Dependent Variable	Model	Independent Variable	Coefficient	t-Statistic
Average Minimum	Institutional	CONSTANT	6.416	26.693
		E(1)	-.656	-6.811
		R(1)	.013	5.522
	Causal	CONSTANT	4.124	5.727
		E(1)	.090	.849
< 3 Miles	Institutional	CONSTANT	38.520	12.765
		E(1)	4.518	3.735
		R(1)	-.145	-5.056
	Causal	CONSTANT	56.409	5.812
		E(1)	-2.750	-1.925
< 7 Miles	Institutional	CONSTANT	66.831	29.747
		E(1)	1.797	1.996
		R(1)	-.033	-1.554
	Causal	CONSTANT	67.307	11.700
		E(1)	.684	.807

Table G-III

Comparison of Summary Statistics for Piecewise Institutional Models
Downtown Los Angeles, 1935-79

Dependent Variable	1st Knot	2nd Knot	Adjusted R²	Critical F Value	F Value For Model	Durban-Watson Statistic
Average Minimum	1944	1968	.661	16.519	22.480	1.844
	1948	1968	.653	15.216	21.720	1.831
	1956	1968	.628	11.505	19.560	1.649
	1944	1964	.610	9.128	18.180	1.580
	1948	1964	.609	9.003	18.130	1.610
	1956	1964	.606	8.629	17.930	1.546
	1960	1968	.599	7.781	17.450	1.567
	1940	1968	.579	5.511	16.100	1.491
< 3 Miles	1968	1974	.503	8.612	12.140	1.323
	1964	1974	.492	7.559	11.640	1.214
< 7 Miles	1968	1974	.196	7.114	3.680	1.408
	1956	1968	.191	6.823	3.600	1.424
	1956	1964	.177	6.027	3.370	1.389

Table G-IV
Piecewise Institutional Model, Downtown Los Angeles, 1935-79
Average Minimum Daily Visibility

1st Knot	2nd Knot	Independent Variable	Coefficient	t-Statistic
1944	1968	CONSTANT	6.586	28.913
		E(1)	-.176	-1.267
		R(1)	-.047	-2.756
		R(2)	.049	3.192
		R(3)	.019	3.635
1948	1968	CONSTANT	6.576	28.459
		E(1)	-.181	-1.257
		R(1)	-.056	-2.658
		R(2)	.058	3.003
		R(3)	.020	3.720
1956	1968	CONSTANT	6.487	27.800
		E(1)	-.884	-4.619
		R(1)	.028	3.000
		R(2)	-.022	-2.382
		R(3)	.022	3.627
1944	1964	CONSTANT	6.554	26.443
		E(1)	-.080	-.417
		R(1)	-.054	-2.647
		R(2)	.052	3.014
		R(3)	.015	2.484
1948	1964	CONSTANT	6.544	26.495
		E(1)	-.016	-.076
		R(1)	-.072	-2.727
		R(2)	.066	3.000
		R(3)	.017	2.782
1956	1964	CONSTANT	6.466	26.898
		E(1)	-.912	-4.603
		R(1)	.032	3.176
		R(2)	-.036	-2.941
		R(3)	.026	3.198
1960	1968	CONSTANT	6.415	26.629
		E(1)	-.692	-4.225
		R(1)	.016	2.436
		R(2)	-.012	-1.553
		R(3)	.023	3.160
1940	1968	CONSTANT	6.480	15.670
		E(1)	-.458	-3.598
		R(1)	-.204	-.559
		R(2)	.210	.578
		R(3)	.016	2.784

Table G-V
Piecewise Institutional Model, Downtown Los Angeles, 1935-79
Percent Days Minimum Visibility < 3 Miles

1st Knot	2nd Knot	Independent Variable	Coefficient	t-Statistic
1968	1974	CONSTANT	38.812	13.740
		E(1)	4.243	3.102
		R(1)	-.130	-3.274
		R(2)	-.354	-2.163
		R(3)	.606	3.044
1964	1974	CONSTANT	39.493	13.283
		E(1)	3.132	1.741
		R(1)	-.078	-1.211
		R(2)	-.173	-1.918
		R(3)	.350	3.151

Table G-VI
Piecewise Institutional Model, Downtown Los Angeles, 1935-79
Percent Days Minimum Visibility < 7 Miles

1st Knot	2nd Knot	Independent Variable	Coefficient	t-Statistic
1968	1974	CONSTANT	68.265	31.937
		E(1)	.146	.141
		R(1)	.029	.975
		R(2)	-.378	-3.059
		R(3)	.397	2.637
1956	1968	CONSTANT	65.359	28.575
		E(1)	5.073	2.705
		R(1)	-.229	-2.496
		R(2)	.234	2.589
		R(3)	-.148	-2.503
1956	1964	CONSTANT	65.517	28.356
		E(1)	5.286	2.776
		R(1)	-.256	-2.670
		R(2)	.338	2.852
		R(3)	-.179	-2.337

APPENDIX H
Best Institutional Models
Visibility Data 1950-82

Table H-I

Best Institutional Models of Visibility Data, 1950-82

Location	County Source Activity	Mobile (Vehicles)	Stationary (Employment)	Institutional Variable
Downtown Los Angeles				
Average Minimum	Los Angeles	Personal	Total	Total
< 3 Miles	Los Angeles	Personal	Total	Personal Autos
< 7 Miles	Los Angeles	All	Total	All Vehicles
Los Angeles International Airport				
< 7 Miles (FAA)	Los Angeles	All	Total	All Vehicles
< 3 Miles (FAA)	Los Angeles	Personal	Total	Personal Autos
< 3 Miles (Keith)	Los Angeles	Personal	Total	Personal Autos
Burbank	Los Angeles	All	Total	All Vehicles
Long Beach	Orange	All	Total	All Vehicles
Riverside	Orange	All	Total	All Vehicles
San Bernardino	Riverside/San Bernardino	All	Manufacturing	Manufacturing Employment

Table H-II

Summary Statistics for Best Institutional Models, 1950-82

Location & Dependent Variable	Adjusted R^2	Critical F Value	F Value for Model	Durban-Watson Statistic
Downtown Los Angeles				
Average Minimum	.970	11.267	26.120	1.476
< 3 Miles	.697	5.749	9.180	1.652
< 7 Miles	.970	13.000	7.370	1.822
Los Angeles International Airport				
< 7 Miles (FAA)	.937	6.746	7.950	1.925
< 3 Miles (FAA)	.776	15.290	14.150	1.986
< 3 Miles (Keith)	.536	8.062	25.630	1.335
Burbank	.763	55.797	31.610	.951
Long Beach	.822	8.961	34.620	1.328
Riverside	.862	6.935	5.940	1.924
San Bernardino	.816	14.815	22.300	1.624

Table H-III

Econometric Results for Best Institutional Models, 1950-82

Location and Dependent Variable	Independent Variable	Coefficient	t-Statistic
Downtown LA Average Minimum	CONSTANT	6.598	4.346
	M(1)	-.192	-.624
	S(1)	-.779	-1.086
	R(1)	.078	3.549
Downtown LA < 3 Miles	CONSTANT	45.253	1.808
	M(1)	-4.997	-.920
	S(1)	10.250	1.494
	R(1)	-.733	-2.647
Downtown LA < 7 Miles	CONSTANT	23.464	1.391
	M(1)	6.045	1.759
	S(1)	28.403	2.086
	R(1)	-.431	-3.689
LAX < 7 Miles (FAA)	CONSTANT	26.962	2.272
	M(1)	1.674	.620
	S(1)	10.346	.906
	R(1)	-.259	-2.810
LAX < 3 Miles (FAA)	CONSTANT	7.630	1.335
	M(1)	-.256	-.186
	S(1)	3.434	1.802
	R(1)	-.259	-4.112
LAX < 3 Miles (Keith)	CONSTANT	38.698	2.962
	M(1)	-4.011	-1.593
	S(1)	2.973	.855
	R(1)	-.425	-3.054
Burbank < 3 Miles	CONSTANT	-16.269	-.753
	M(1)	12.283	3.183
	S(1)	12.987	.772
	R(1)	-.879	-7.664
Long Beach < 3 Miles	CONSTANT	37.489	4.387
	M(1)	9.226	.824
	S(1)	7.820	.153
	R(1)	-1.284	-3.201
Riverside < 3 Miles	CONSTANT	16.439	1.679
	M(1)	23.572	1.837
	S(1)	30.385	.519
	R(1)	-1.317	-2.866
San Bernardino < 3 Miles	CONSTANT	16.121	.968
	M(1)	19.460	.937
	S(1)	774.487	2.920
	R(1)	-60.183	-4.035

Table H-IV
Piecewise Institutional Models that Improve Over Base Model

1ˢᵗ Knot	2ⁿᵈ Knot	County Source Activity	Mobile Source	Stationary Source	Institutional Variable
Los Angeles International Airport (Keith) < 3 Miles					
1960	1974	Los Angeles	Personal Autos	Total Employment	Personal Autos
1964	1974	Los Angeles	Personal Autos	Total Employment	Personal Autos
1974		Los Angeles	Personal Autos	Total Employment	Personal Autos
1956	1974	Los Angeles	Personal Autos	Total Employment	Personal Autos
1968	1974	Los Angeles	Personal Autos	Total Employment	Personal Autos
Burbank Airport < 3 Miles					
1960	1968	Los Angeles	All Vehicles	Total Employment	All Vehicles
1956	1968	Los Angeles	All Vehicles	Total Employment	All Vehicles
1968		Los Angeles	All Vehicles	Total Employment	All Vehicles
San Bernardino < 3 Miles					
1968	1974	Riverside/San Bernardino	All Vehicles	Manufacturing Employment	Manufacturing Employment
1968	1976	Riverside/San Bernardino	All Vehicles	Manufacturing Employment	Manufacturing Employment

Table H-V
Summary Statistics for Piecewise Institutional Models that Improve Over Base Model

1ˢᵗ Knot	2ⁿᵈ Knot	Adjusted R^2	Critical F Value	F Value for Model	Durban-Watson Statistic
Los Angeles International Airport (Keith) < 3 Miles					
1960	1974	.715	8.479	29.150	1.937
1964	1974	.667	5.311	24.140	1.698
1974		.646	8.701	27.750	1.559
1956	1974	.640	3.900	21.940	1.582
1968	1974	.638	3.804	21.740	1.563
Burbank < 3 Miles					
1960	1968	.831	5.432	29.300	1.187
1956	1968	.811	3.429	25.670	1.090
1968		.810	6.926	31.500	1.029
San Bernardino < 3 Miles					
1968	1974	.854	3.514	18.760	1.997
1968	1976	.854	3.514	18.830	2.106

Table H-VI
Results of Piecewise Institutional Models that Improve Over Base Model

1st Knot	2nd Knot	Independent Variable	Coefficient	t-Statistic
LA International Airport (Keith) < 3 Miles				
1960	1974	CONSTANT	33.129	2.755
		R(1)	-3.746	-3.431
		R(2)	2.991	2.793
		R(3)	.813	3.666
		M(1)	5.315	1.844
		S(1)	1.486	.538
1964	1974	CONSTANT	21.406	1.751
		R(1)	-1.337	-3.346
		R(2)	.637	1.659
		R(3)	.753	3.131
		M(1)	4.739	1.476
		S(1)	1.204	.403
1974		CONSTANT	21.672	1.719
		R(1)	-.722	-4.708
		R(2)	.784	3.173
		M(1)	2.555	.847
		S(1)	1.386	.451
1956	1974	CONSTANT	33.670	1.621
		R(1)	-5.329	-.845
		R(2)	4.596	.730
		R(3)	.795	3.184
		M(1)	2.997	.966
		S(1)	1.463	.472
1968	1974	CONSTANT	20.575	1.595
		R(1)	-.848	-3.156
		R(2)	.160	.576
		R(3)	.736	2.788
		M(1)	3.320	.997
		S(1)	1.387	.445

1st Knot	2nd Knot	Independent Variable	Coefficient	t-Statistic
Burbank < 3 Miles				
1960	1968	CONSTANT	30.947	1.363
		R(1)	-3.395	-1.993
		R(2)	3.816	2.132
		R(3)	-1.317	-3.611
		M(1)	4.673	1.079
		S(1)	9.627	.674
1956	1968	CONSTANT	39.013	1.110
		R(1)	-9.956	-1.096
		R(2)	10.141	1.115
		R(3)	-1.054	-2.958
		M(1)	4.220	.923
		S(1)	10.183	.673
1968		CONSTANT	7.601	.360
		R(1)	.156	.412
		R(2)	-1.010	-2.840
		M(1)	3.778	.826
		S(1)	8.936	.589
San Bernardino < 3 Miles				
1968	1974	CONSTANT	28.210	1.772
		R(1)	-48.464	-1.635
		R(2)	27.926	1.050
		R(3)	-44.877	-2.869
		M(1)	2.830	.139
		S(1)	600.738	2.092
1968	1976	CONSTANT	35.070	2.142
		R(1)	-39.310	-1.351
		R(2)	27.447	1.040
		R(3)	-43.676	-2.887
		M(1)	2.608	.128
		S(1)	434.190	1.489

For Product Safety Concerns and Information please contact our EU
representative GPSR@taylorandfrancis.com Taylor & Francis Verlag GmbH,
Kaufingerstraße 24, 80331 München, Germany

Printed and bound by CPI Group (UK) Ltd, Croydon, CR0 4YY
08/05/2025
01864445-0002